BOREAL TIES

Winter 2002
December 17th

To Maria Paulinas
Best Wishes .... Enjoy a Journey
to Greenland with my Grandfather

[signature]

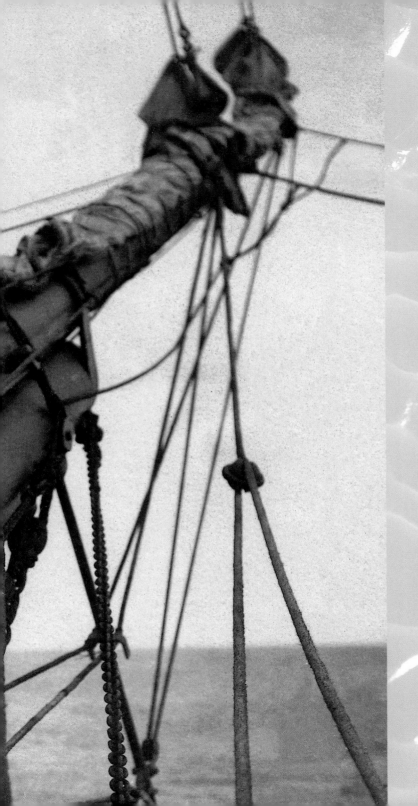

BOREAL TIES

PHOTOGRAPHS AND TWO DIARIES OF
THE 1901 PEARY RELIEF EXPEDITION

EDITED BY

Kim Fairley Gillis

AND

Silas Hibbard Ayer III

UNIVERSITY OF NEW MEXICO PRESS
ALBUQUERQUE

Erik icebound in Melville Bay pack (B179)

"We now left civilization and sailed for Cape York on Melville Bay known as the graveyard of Arctic ships." (Bement Notes)

PREVIOUS SPREAD:

The guests on the bowsprit (B29/W52) FAC

l. to r. Herbert Berri, Limond Stone, Louis Bement, Clarence Wyckoff, and Alfred Church.

October 10, 1909
En route to Milwaukee

My dear Bement,

*I have read with much interest the long
letter which you have sent me. Such
appreciation and such a friendly attitude
by one who is in a neutral position as you
are is a very high compliment. Some day
in the near future, I hope to get to Ithaca
and then we will renew our boreal ties.*

Frederick A. Cook

In memory of
Betty Wyckoff Pfann Balderston

Icebergs (W263/B234)

CONTENTS

ACKNOWLEDGMENTS

It is difficult to say when we came up with the idea for this book. It was born out of a lifetime of interest in the Arctic and two families' desire to do something with the material. We are not experts in the history of exploration, the history of photography, or Arctic cultures. We pored, however, through countless books, letters, and microfilm; we studied thousands of photographs. And we consulted professionals in the field of photography, anthropology, geology, and Arctic history, without whom this book would never have been possible.

We are grateful to the people from the George Eastman House International Museum of Photography and Film, who offered their time and expertise. Joe Struble enthusiastically reviewed the photographs and gave valuable insight. Mark Osterman shared his vast knowledge of printing and the history of photographic processes. Todd Gustavson identified cameras from the minutest details in grainy or blurry enlargements. Gary Albright thoughtfully viewed photograph upon photograph, pointing out important elements that characterized them, and helped narrow down the film, papers, and processes of the photographs, all so crucial in understanding the collections.

We would like to thank the people at Foto 1 Photographic and Digital Imaging, especially Michelle Romano who spent many weeks scanning hundreds of images. Jasmine Alinder, Visiting Assistant Professor of Art History; Joanne Leonard and Carol Jacobsen, Professors of Art at the University of Michigan, made many valuable suggestions. Elaine Engst, University Archivist and Director of the Division of Rare and Manuscript Collections, Cornell University Library, helped with the Alfred W. Church and Edward G. Wyckoff collections at the Cornell University Library. Dayle Connolly of the National

Archives at College Park, Maryland, and Laura Kissel, Polar Curator at the Byrd Polar Research Center Archival Program, The Ohio State University, offered their time and much needed material. Leif Vanggaard of the Danish Arctic Institute and Bjarne Pedersen, Acting High Commissioner of Greenland, supplied information on the history of Greenland. Cecil H. "Jack" Hull helped with ship and navigational questions. Tara Berry and Gary Dorsey provided direction related to publishing.

We owe a great deal of thanks to Carol Cooperrider who created a beautiful map. We also thank Richard James of Ann Arbor, Michigan, who supplied us with base maps, and Timothy Utter, of the University of Michigan Map Library who helped with many thoughtful suggestions.

We are profoundly grateful to the Frederick A. Cook Society for their generous financial contribution to our project. We also would like to thank Beverly Brannon, Curator of the Prints & Photographs Reading Room, who sat for long hours assisting us with the Cook photographs at the Library of Congress.

George and Lana Pfann were most giving of their time and very generously loaned us the bulk of Clarence Wyckoff's original papers. And Joan Niles Sears delighted us with heartrending memories of "Freddie" Church, which helped us in researching his life.

This book became a reality thanks to the tireless support of our spouses, Mike Gillis and Betsy Ayer, as well as David Peters, David Ayer, Marija Freeland, Lucy Silverio, and Susan Sharp who listened endlessly and read the manuscript countless times, providing thoughtful suggestions and much needed encouragement. We would like to thank all of the people from the University of New Mexico Press, especially David Holtby and Robyn Mundy, who made the process seem so easy.

Finally, we owe our greatest thanks to Betty Wyckoff Pfann Balderston, who brought us together and gave us the inspiration to collaborate on this interesting and exciting project. For years she urged us to get together. We finally did, in 1999 at the National Archives in Washington, D.C. There, our "boreal ties" were renewed, and the goal of two families to preserve and share their rich collections was at last realized.

Kim Fairley Gillis
Chelsea, Michigan

Silas Hibbard Ayer III
Ellicott City, Maryland

EDITORIAL NOTE

Written on board the SS *Erik,* the Wyckoff-Bement diaries began as a collection of notes mixed with observations about geography, water temperatures, and weather patterns. When the men returned from the expedition, they rewrote many of their diary entries. Louis Bement rewrote the first few pages from 7 July–29 July, 1901. Clarence Wyckoff rewrote most of his entries, then dictated them to his daughter, Barbara, who recorded them in shorthand, and transcribed them several decades later. Wyckoff's entries from August 14–31, many of them brief phrases, were missing from his daughter's rewritten draft so we transcribed them from the original.

A few of Wyckoff's comments in his original diary were deleted from his daughter's final transcript. In the same way, Bement removed some of his original remarks when he rewrote early entries in his diary. The reasons for these deletions in either man's final diary are uncertain. For this book we have included those deleted entries in italics.

Some difficulty arises in determining the correct spelling of Inuit and place names at the turn of the twentieth century. Several spellings from 1901 changed in the following years depending on the authors recording them, and in a few cases the earlier names are no longer preferred. To complicate matters, for some of the place names Wyckoff and Bement used as many as four different spellings.

In the diaries we decided to leave misspelled place names exactly as Wyckoff and Bement recorded them. In creating the map and index, where the Wyckoff and Bement spellings are similar to the present form, we listed only the present form, based on the *Geographic Names Database (GNDB)*, National Imagery and Mapping Agency, United States Board of

ELLESMERE ISLAND

Payer Harbor
Cape Sabine
Herschel Bay

Cairn Point

Smith Sound

Anoratuk (Anoritôq)

Etah

GREENLAND

78°

Nerke (Neqe)
Igloodahomyne (Igdluluarssuit)
Kookan (Kûgat)

Robertson Bay

Anniversary Lodge

McCormick Bay
Red Cliff

HAKLUYT ISLAND

HERBERT ISLAND

Inglefield Gulf

Salmon River

NORTHUMBERLAND ISLAND

Whale Sound

Otrik Bay

+ Hawk Mountain
(Mt. Gyrfalco)

Netiulumi (Natsilivik)

CAREY ISLANDS

Wolstenholme Sound

Dalrymple Rock

+ Mount Dundas

Thule

Petowik Glacier

76°

0   50 km.
0   50 miles

Cape York

72°   68°

Cape Clarence
Wyckoff

0   1,000 km
0   500 miles

Fort Conger

ELLESMERE ISLAND

Detail Map

GREENLAND

Melville Bay

Baffin Bay

Upernavik

DISKO ISLAND

Godhavn

80°

Arctic Circle

70°

Frederickshaab

Cape Farewell

Saglek Bay

Labrador Sea

60°

LABRADOR

Domino Run

Strait of Belle Isle

NEWFOUNDLAND

St. John's

CANADA

50°

Gulf of St. Lawrence

Port aux Basques

N. Sydney

NOVA SCOTIA

Carleton Island

U.S.

Halifax

Yarmouth

Boston

Ithaca

New York City

Atlantic Ocean

110° 90° 70° 50°

Geographic Names. In cases where the 1901 spelling differs significantly from the present form, we listed the early standard spelling based on Dan Laursen's *The Place Names of North Greenland,* (København: C. A. Reitzels Forlag, 1972), followed by the present form. For instance, the modern settlement of Igdluluarssuit was in 1901 spelled Igloodahomyne. Wyckoff spelled it Igloo doo hominy and Bement spelled it Igloodehominy. So although we retained Wyckoff and Bement's spelling in the diaries, the map and index will show the settlement as Igloodahomyne [Igdluluarssuit].

We treated Inuit spellings in a similar manner. The diaries retain the Wyckoff and Bement spellings, however, for captions we used the more common spelling listed in Hugh Lee's "Census of the Smith-Sound Eskimos, August 31, 1895" as published in Robert Peary's *Northward Over the 'Great Ice',* vol. 1 (511–14). Some people find the word *Eskimo* offensive because it translates as 'eaters of raw flesh.' We used the names preferred by the native northern Greenlanders themselves, which are *Inuk* [singular/person] and *Inuit* [plural/people].

As much as possible we attempted to preserve the original form of the diaries. With the exception of expanding abbreviations, and correcting punctuation, the Bement and Wyckoff entries were collated and printed verbatim. Whenever there were two versions of the same entry for an author, the more detailed (usually later version) of the two was selected. Unbracketed italicized sections indicate portions included in the original but omitted from the rewritten versions. Brackets are used for interpolated editorial additions to improve readability. Although they overlap in some places, the daily entries were printed in their entirety to compare and contrast the perspectives of the two men who were close friends yet very different in personality and ten years apart in age.

In addition to offering a unique perspective, Bement's photograph log provided subject and place names, which helped us to identify the images. As with the diaries, the photographs, though enlarged, have been reproduced as close to their original as possible, with minimal cropping and retouching.

With the exception of the images loaned to us by the Cornell University Library, the photographs remain privately owned. In the cases where an identical image can be found in two collections, each collection number has been cited with the first indicating the one reproduced here. Abbreviations shown to the right indicate the various collections.

Following some of the illustrations are quotations. Those from the Bement Notes, or Bement Log, are found in the private collection of the Ayer family, and the Wyckoff Notes are contained in the private collection of the George and Bruce Pfann families. The abbreviation FAC represents those images stamped "Copyright 1901 by Dr. F. A. Cook."

Key to photographic collections

[W]   Wyckoff photograph album
Private collection of the Gillis family

[K]   Keystone glass positives
Private collection of the Gillis family

[B]   Bement papers and photographs
Private collection of the Ayer family.

[C]   Alfred Whiting Church photograph album, [1910?]
Division of Rare and Manuscript Collection, Cornell University Library

[E]   Edward Guild Wyckoff papers, 1899–1910
Division of Rare and Manuscript Collection, Cornell University Library

[P]   Wyckoff papers and photographs
Private collection of the George and Bruce Pfann families

INTRODUCTION

INTRODUCTION

In the summer of 1901, a relief ship set sail for the remote region of northwestern Greenland in search of the famed Arctic explorer, Robert Peary, his wife, Josephine, and their seven-year-old daughter, Marie. Clarence Wyckoff and Louis Bement, two close friends from Ithaca, New York, learned that the *Peary Arctic Club* was looking for members who would contribute financially to the expedition in return for the opportunity to travel on the ship as possibly the very first Arctic tourists. Though they realized there were risks associated with Arctic travel, Wyckoff and Bement believed the expedition, with its backing by the *Peary Arctic Club,* would employ an experienced crew and provide the most modern tools and equipment. They jumped at the chance. They went for an exotic experience, envisioning themselves as typical tourists, hunting wild game, catching a glimpse of an iceberg or two, and relaxing from the stresses of everyday life.

What they actually experienced was far more than they ever expected. Thirty years later, in recalling the three months in 1901, Wyckoff wrote, "At the end of two weeks all of our meat had been thrown overboard. At the end of three, we had run out of potatoes and all fresh vegetables. When we landed at Sydney, we had less than a barrel of flour, one can of baking powder and practically nothing besides beans, dried peas and what the sailors called salt horse." In addition to their gruesome diet, the diary

Louis Bement, 1901 (B357)

Robert Peary, Mrs. Peary, and
Dr. Cook (W123/B49)
Red Cliff, site of the Peary's former house.

entries of Wyckoff and Bement reveal their outrage over the hives, maggots, and head lice that plagued them. They experienced unimaginable difficulties when ice forced their ship up and onto its side. And on more than one occasion, they risked their lives because of the crew's incompetence. In spite of their hardship and unaware of the importance of their record to future generations, Wyckoff and Bement documented their experience with a measure of skill and detachment.

Today their photographs and diary entries shift us back to a time before the discussion of Arctic exploration invoked bitter passion. They contain images of the celebrated Arctic explorers, Robert Peary, Matthew Henson, and Dr. Frederick Cook, taken eight years before the storm of controversy over who reached the North Pole first. In 1909, when Robert Peary and Matthew Henson announced they reached the North Pole, and they learned that Dr. Frederick Cook claimed he beat them to the Pole by one year, hostility between the men erupted.[1] Robert Peary and his supporters launched a national campaign to discredit Dr. Cook and Cook launched his own campaign to defend himself. Unfortunately, the subsequent conflict became so brutal that it turned the men into bitter enemies.

One of the most valuable aspects of this collection from the 1901 expedition is that it offers a fresh glimpse of these very famous Arctic explorers, their character, their strengths and their weaknesses, through the impartial eyes of two men who had no idea of what lay ahead.

The *Peary Arctic Club*

The 1901 material tenders a unique view of the early days of the *Peary Arctic Club*. From its organization in 1898 to the height of its power during the early years of the Peary-Cook controversy, the *Peary Arctic Club* served as Robert Peary's foundation for exploration.[2] As a part of its scientific and philanthropic effort, the club asked its members, who were among the country's wealthiest businessmen, to pay $1,000 a

---

1.   Andrew A. Freeman. *The Case for Doctor Cook* (New York: Coward-McCann, Inc., 1961), 153–57.
2.   Ibid., 64.

year, for four years, to support Robert Peary in his Arctic work. The club provided Peary with the supplies he needed and in return for their support, he supplied them with valuable Inuit art and artifacts. Robert Peary also named newly discovered geographical points after many of his supporters in the *Peary Arctic Club*.[3]

In the summer of 1899, less than six months after its organization, the *Peary Arctic Club* sent its secretary, Herbert Bridgman, to northern Greenland on a relief ship, *Diana*. When he arrived, Mr. Bridgman learned that all but three of Robert Peary's toes had been frozen and had required amputation.[4] Mr. Bridgman urged Mr. Peary to return on the *Diana* so that he could receive treatment from a specialist, but he refused to leave.

Shortly thereafter, Herbert Bridgman delivered a letter from Peary to his wife, Josephine. The news of her husband's suffering alarmed her greatly and she immediately began making plans to travel north. She believed that if Herbert Bridgman could not convince her husband to return for proper medical treatment, she could. In July of 1900 Mrs. Peary and her daughter, Marie, departed on the SS *Windward,* which was the next relief expedition organized by the *Peary Arctic Club*.[5] By the end of the fall of 1900, when the *Windward* failed to return, and still no word arrived from Robert Peary himself, his supporters became concerned. In addition to finding Robert Peary, they felt they needed to locate Mrs. Peary and her daughter.

To finance a third expedition, the *Peary Arctic Club* conceived the idea of asking its members with more than a casual interest in polar exploration to donate an additional $500 for the right to travel on the *Erik* as a guest of the club.[6] Assuming the *Erik* would find the Peary family, it would deliver additional supplies, a physician would provide any necessary medical help, and the men would return with a detailed report to the club. The *Peary Arctic Club* also gave the men the difficult task of

Herbert L. Bridgman, Commander of the *Erik* (W13)

"He stated that we should buy no food that he had arranged for everything. . . . On the way north to North Sidney . . . we stopped overnight in Halifax and . . . ordered a quantity of delicacies such as figs, dates, olives, sardines, and Hylers candy. This was a fortunate move as before we got back we were living on this private supply." (Wyckoff Notes)

3. Theodore Roosevelt, "Letter of Appreciation to Commander Robert E. Peary," *The National Geographic Magazine* 14 (1903): 330.
4. Herbert Bridgman, "Ten Years of the Peary Arctic Club," *The National Geographic Magazine* 19 (1908): 663.
5. Ibid., 663.
6. Treasurer's Report-Peary Arctic Club, 11 March–December 1901, Edward Guild Wyckoff Papers, Division of Rare and Manuscript Collections, Cornell University Library, Ithaca, New York (hereafter cited as [E]).

Mrs. Josephine D. Peary (B44/W3)

" . . . who has wintered three times in the Arctic within 700–600 miles from the Pole and enjoys it. Peary owes much of his success to her assistance." (Bement Log)

delivering word to Mr. Peary of the death of his mother in Portland, Maine. In a confidential report to its members, the *Peary Arctic Club*'s secretary, Herbert Bridgman wrote:

> The summer of 1901 is likely to mark the culmination of the work of the Peary Club, though its members, confident as they have been from the outset in Mr. Peary's success, are pledged to stand by him unfalteringly to the end. Three years have elapsed since Mr. Peary left America, and two full seasons' work is to be learned upon the return of the Erik. More interesting, in a personal and dramatic way, than the geographic work of Mr. Peary, is the fate of his wife and daughter and of the steamer Windward from which nothing has been heard since her departure from Godhavn, Greenland, August 20, 1900.[7]

As one of the *Peary Arctic Club*'s youngest and strongest supporters, Clarence Wyckoff approached the second relief expedition with great enthusiasm. Wyckoff's father was William O. Wyckoff, who started the first typewriter manufacturing company that eventually became Remington Typewriter.[8] He died in 1895 when Clarence was nineteen, leaving him with more than a million-dollar inheritance. After attending Cornell University, Clarence worked with his brother, Edward, a builder, who was developing an area of Ithaca, New York, known as Cornell Heights. The two brothers bought controlling interests in the Booth's Hyomei Company, which manufactured patent medicine. In 1899, Clarence took over the management of Booth's Hyomei, and by the following year, he started another venture, the C. F. Wyckoff Company, which sold newspaper advertising.

Throughout this time of investing capital and managing various businesses, Clarence Wyckoff followed the work of Robert Peary through confidential correspondence he received as a member of the *Peary Arctic Club*. To Wyckoff, the 1901 expedition was a tremendous departure from his daily routine of business meetings

---

7.   Confidential Report to the Members of the Peary Arctic Club, 12 June 1901, [E].
8.   Carol Sisler, *Enterprising Families Ithaca New York: Their Houses and Businesses* (Ithaca: Enterprise Publishing, 1986), 87–88.

The Bement Family (B355)

From top: Louis Bement, Addie (Taber) Bement, and daughters, Ariel, Norma, and Lucie.

and time-consuming social engagements. He jumped at the opportunity to actively participate in an important relief mission where he could learn firsthand about Robert Peary's Arctic work.

Wyckoff easily convinced two of his friends to go along as well. When he casually mentioned to a group of business associates that he planned to go on an Arctic expedition and that he could take one person as his guest, Louis Bement immediately answered, "I'll go."[9] At the age of thirty-five with a wife and three daughters, Bement had sold men's hats and caps for the Henry H. Angell Company for eight years.[10] He was at a point in his life when he was considering a career change. A trip to the Arctic would give him some time to assess his future. He embraced the thrill of meeting Inuit, learning their customs and lifestyle, and avoiding three hot summer months in New York while spending time in one of the coldest regions on earth.

Clarence talked his friend, Alfred Church, a Chi Psi fraternity brother at Cornell, into going along as well. Church was the grandson of Gail Borden, who invented a process to condense milk and subsequently founded the Borden Milk Company.[11] He studied mechanical engineering at Cornell and was about to graduate. Like Wyckoff and Bement, Church saw the expedition as a rare opportunity that arrived at the perfect time in his life.

Five paying guests of the *Peary Arctic Club* boarded the *Erik:* Clarence Wyckoff, Louis "Louie" Bement, Alfred "Fred" Church, Herbert Berri, and Limond Stone. Herbert Berri was the son of William Berri who owned Brooklyn's *The Standard Union* newspaper and Limond Stone was Herbert Berri's professor at the Polytechnic Institute in New York.[12] Because of concerns about Robert Peary's state of health, the *Peary Arctic Club* hired Dr. Frederick Cook as surgeon and second in command for the 1901 expedition. Dr. Cook was the surgeon of the first Peary expedition of 1891 and the Belgian Antarctic Expedition of 1897.[13] He planned to treat Robert Peary if necessary, but he also hoped to continue his ethnological studies of the

9. Obituary, *Ithaca Journal-News,* 27 February 1933.
10. *Manning's Ithaca Directories,* 1884–1901, s.v. "Bement."
11. Joe B. Frantz, *Gail Borden: Dairyman to a Nation* (Norman: University of Oklahoma Press, c.1951), 216–61.
12. Confidential Report to the Members of the Peary Arctic Club, 12 June 1901, [E].
13. Freeman, *The Case for Dr. Cook,* 13–15, 50–58.

Commander (W159) FAC

Herbert Bridgman

Physician and Second in Command (W125)

Dr. Frederick Cook

Captain (W12)

John Blakeney

First Mate (W58)

Moses Bartlett

Second Mate (W95)

William Bartlett

Chief Engineer (W41)

Fullerton

Engineer (W99)

George Wardwell

Guest (W8)

Professor Limond C. Stone

Guest (B352/W6)

Louis C. Bement

Guest (B350/W10)

Clarence F. Wyckoff

Guest (B351/W5)

Alfred W. Church

Guest (W7)

Herbert Berri

people of northern Greenland. Herbert Bridgman, a journalist with *The Standard Union,* and the secretary of the *Peary Arctic Club,* went along as the commander.

There was growing public interest in Arctic exploration in 1901 and, in particular, great interest in the Peary family. For that reason, there was a need for secrecy on the *Erik.* The men received confidential reports from the *Peary Arctic Club* before the expedition and the club asked them to keep private all of their personal family contact related to Peary's work. With only the use of the telegraph at a few planned stops along the route, it was easy for intimate conversation among family members to become public knowledge. In his diary from the expedition, Bement wrote a telling page of code words, which he used to protect his privacy in sending telegrams to his wife. He chose code names based on people he knew in his own family. A few examples were:

CODE	MEANING
Helen	Peary came back with us
Ralph	Peary is on way back
Frank	Peary is dead
Burt	Mrs. Peary and girl all okay
Pete	Mrs. Peary and girl not found
Will	Read telegram in Clarence's office

Although the guests of the *Peary Arctic Club* knew that Arctic travel could be perilous and unpredictable, they believed they were traveling on a modern ship with the benefit of modern tools and equipment. Technically a chartered steamer, the SS *Erik* was chosen by the *Peary Arctic Club* because it was "thoroughly overhauled and refitted" and it was "certified by the highest marine authority in London to be in the best condition and well adapted for her Arctic work."[14] As it turned out, the *Erik*'s condition left much to be desired. Wyckoff, in a 1931 lecture, said, "At the time they [the engines] were built, I imagine they were rather modern, but the ship had seen much hard usage in the Hudson Bay trade and the engines were only useful in

14.   Confidential Report to the Members of The Peary Arctic Club, 12 June 1901, [E].

A beautiful afternoon (W46/B270)

Berri photographs Marie Ahnighito Peary and unknown Inuk woman wearing Inuit winter costume. "To be prepared for all conditions of work in the Arctic regions a number of lenses from the shortest wide angle to a telephoto attachment are indispensable." [Rudolf Kersting, The White World: Life and Adventures Within the Arctic Circle Portrayed by Famous Living Explorers. *(New York: Lewis Scribner & Company, 1902), 238]*

a fair wind. With a fair wind and no sails spread, we could make about 6 or 7 miles an hour. When the wind or tide was against us, we anchored or tied up to a cake of ice."[15] Besides their surprise in discovering the true condition of the ship, Wyckoff and Bement recorded their reactions to the lack of organization behind the expedition. As paying guests of the club, the men expected certain basic living conditions. Much to their dismay, it became nearly impossible to hire an adequate crew, and as they reported in their diaries, they eventually signed on as able-bodied seamen performing ordinary sailor duties aboard ship.

Photographic Equipment

Since Wyckoff and Bement worked all day assisting the captain or supervising the meals, they found themselves taking photographs as a leisure activity. During off duty hours and peak conditions, as many as six men took photographs. During poor weather or crises, photography was practically nonexistent.

They took numerous prints seconds apart, but from slightly different perspectives. The men shared with each other their best photographs,[16] and possibly even their cameras, so with the exception of those stamped "Copyright 1901 by Dr. F. A. Cook" it is difficult to determine the photographer in every case.

The photographs of Wyckoff and Bement vary greatly in quality depending on environmental factors and whether they properly washed, fixed, and in some cases, mounted the prints on album pages. Bement's family removed his photographs from the original album in an effort to protect them. Wyckoff chose to crop the corners of several of his photographs, or cut them in oval or circular shapes for stylistic reasons.

The photographs represent a variety of negative, paper, and processing types because of the competing technologies in all areas of photography at the time.[17] By

Dr. Frederick Cook (W125)

15. Personal notes, private collection, George and Bruce Pfann families.
16. Many of the photographs have the names Berri, Stone, Wyckoff, Bement, Church, or Cook penciled on the back as though they were intended to be given to the person.
17. Naomi Rosenblum, *A World History of Photography* (New York: Abbeville Press, 1997), 442–51.

1901, gelatin dry glass plates had been popular for more than two decades on Arctic expeditions.[18] Though it is very difficult to determine from the prints themselves, notes from Wyckoff's diary indicate that he also purchased lactate (rather than gelatin) dry plates for one of his cameras. The advantage of using dry plates was that they could be sensitized with chemicals before the expedition. The men could expose the negatives on the ship, and then store them in light-tight boxes until they were ready for processing.[19] The technical limitation of glass plate photography in 1901 was its hypersensitivity to blue light, making the skies appear over-exposed, and red images appear too dark.

Although their diaries indicate that they made photographic prints while on the ship, their exact film type for any given print is difficult to determine. In addition to glass plates, the Eastman Company produced a daylight loading roll film around 1895[20] and the men experimented with it while on the expedition. Similar to the way we process film today, they could store it on the ship and send it to the company for processing when they returned home.

The 1901 photographs were printed on two types of gelatin emulsion papers: printing-out papers, and developing-out papers. Printing-out papers, also called gelatin-silver-chloride papers, required no chemical development.[21] Considered a contact printing process, it allowed the men to easily print some of the photographs on the ship and check the quality of the images they were taking. They placed the negative and the printing-out paper back to back in a hinged frame and then exposed the frame to sunlight. The hinge made it possible to peel apart the paper and check the quality of the image to measure the necessary amount of sunlight required. Once they achieved a satisfactory image, they fixed the paper with chemicals and completed the process.[22]

18. Douglas Wamsley and William Barr, "Early Photographers of the Canadian Arctic and Greenland," in *Imaging the Arctic*, ed. J. C. H. King (Seattle: University of Washington Press, 1998), 42.
19. Ibid.
20. Ibid.
21. Ibid.
22. William Crawford, *The Keepers of Light: A History & Working Guide to Early Photographic Processes* (New York: Morgan & Morgan, Inc., 1979), 45.

Photography on deck (W97)

l. to r.: Cook, Wyckoff, and Berri. "No dust of any kind is in the atmosphere; it is pure, clear air. It is easy to make good pictures under these conditions, if you study your light. The great difficulty is near the seashore, where with ordinary plates or films, proper exposure is next to an impossibility." (Kersting, The White World, *237)*

Developing-out papers offered more stability and retained the photographs' original appearance longer than printing-out papers. Developing-out papers get warmer as they age and sometimes show signs of silver mirroring, an appearance of a bluish metallic sheen, caused by heat and moisture over time. This seems particularly evident in some of the Wyckoff-Bement photographs. The developing-out papers in this collection have a matte surface and grainier appearance than the printed-out papers. The printed out papers tend to be glossier and slightly purplish in color.[23]

The men employed a variety of cameras. Wyckoff operated a #4 Cartridge Kodak, considered a hand and stand camera for the advanced amateur. It produced 4 x 5 inch images and worked with either roll film or dry glass plates.[24] He also shot twenty-nine panoramic views with the Kodak Panoram #4. Manufactured by Eastman Kodak for the amateur market, the Panoram #4 was simple and easy to use. With a swinging lens, the camera covered an angle of approximately 142 degrees, and Wyckoff printed from several rolls of five exposures.[25] Wyckoff hand cut many of his panoramic views, cropping out portions of white skies in order to easily fit together three photographs per page. Louis Bement used a No. 1A Folding Pocket Kodak that took twelve exposures on quarter-plate daylight loading roll film, producing 2½ x 4¼-inch images.[26]

At the beginning of the expedition, Wyckoff purchased a camera known as a Richard Veriscope to create stereoscopic prints and positive slides for projection. A stereo camera, the Richard Veriscope used two Zeiss lenses and two magazines for dry glass plates. A ground glass attachment focused the camera that mounted on a tripod. When the attachment was replaced with the film and stereo images were taken, it created a scene for each eye so that when superimposed through a viewer, they appeared as a three-dimensional image.[27]

23. James M. Reilly, *Care and Identification of 19th Century Photographic Prints* (Rochester, New York: Eastman Kodak, 1986), 1–13.

24. Michael Auer, *The Illustrated History of the Camera: From 1839 to the Present* (Boston: New York Graphic Society, 1975), 145, 150.

25. Ibid., 269.

26. Ibid., 149.

27. Eaton Lothrop, *A Century of Cameras: From the Collection of the International Museum of Photography at George Eastman House* (New York: Morgan & Morgan, Inc., 1973), 87.

Balancing on the shrouds (w36)

Even with the technological advances made to cameras, film, and developing by 1901, it was no easy matter to produce quality photographs in a region where conditions of light and temperature fluctuated so rapidly. Each of the three processes of taking the photograph, developing the negative, and printing from the negative, was complicated. Developing negatives required the mixing of chemicals and knowledge of processing. Printing the photographs meant exposing the paper and negatives to natural light or exposing them in the ship's darkroom, then washing and fixing the images with chemicals. [28]

Photographic Style

In many ways, the photographic collections of the two men are similar. Each man concentrated a great deal of his energy depicting life on the ship, and each photographed from numerous angles, and during every activity from playing chess to guiding the ship at the wheel. In several photographs, crewmembers smile into the camera, or perform athletic stunts within the picture plane. These photographs testify to the overall friendly rapport between the men.

The images also convey the beauty of the region without excessive sentimentality. The photographs of landscapes and icebergs capture the dramatic light, the vastness, and the isolation of the region. They provide a record of 1901 navigational and hunting equipment, Greenlandic architecture, and traditional clothing. Like modern tourist photographs, their images remind the viewer that the experience was at times fun, relaxing, and an opportunity to witness great beauty.

A number of photographs were set up like studio portraits. With their subjects upright, many in heroic stances, the men chose elements of the ship as props. Some of the images, particularly the formal shots, idealize the explorers. Photographs of Robert Peary show him standing erect, with hands to his sides or behind his back, as he glances off in the distance. They convey self-consciousness and awareness by

28. Crawford, *The Keepers of Light,* 45–48.

Sailors performing stunts on a sledge
while Inuk man fixes the lashings
(B157/W138)

Herbert Berri plays the mandolin while
Bement and others listen (W88/B76)

The Peary Family (W112)

Robert, Josephine, and Marie Ahnighito.

Two Inuit girls at Upernavik (W216)

Peary of the historical importance of the image. It could be argued that they also reflect the vulnerability felt by Peary over his poor physical health at the time.

For formal seated photographs, particularly those in the collection copyrighted by Dr. Cook, the subjects appear in front of canvas or musk ox fur backdrops. The body faces front with the head turned slightly to one side. These formal images concentrate on dramatic lighting and composition, and closely resemble daguerreotype portraiture of the mid-nineteenth century.[29]

The differences in their photographic styles reflect the interests and personalities of the men. Wyckoff posed and formally arranged his Inuit subjects. He photographed them at a middle distance with their expressions clearly showing discomfort or reluctance at being photographed. With his camera aimed mostly upward to figures positioned on rocks, Wyckoff elevated his subjects in the viewfinder. This may reflect a veneration of the Inuit, but it also implies a lack of familiarity with his subject.

Bement's photographs suggest more of an intimacy with his Inuit subjects. He photographed many of them at a closer range and in settings that were more natural. His images convey a human relationship between people, with scenes of mothers holding their babies, girls holding hands, and families gathered together. They represent a wide variety of emotion exhibiting everything from smiles to frowns, and warmth to suspicion. Bement's photographs also focus on the Inuit lifestyle. His images capture Inuit in everyday activities such as hunting walrus and caribou, preparing and eating meat, and tanning and sewing skins. His choice of images underscores his respect and regard for Inuit culture.

A couple of Bement's photographs of a boy and young mother show the subjects naked or partially clothed. One photograph of a sleeping woman, and another of a man pointing his camera into the woman's tupik (tent), clearly seem intrusive. Although the mother appears a willing participant in the photographic process, in a relaxed stance and even smiling, the fact that the boy hides his genitals may suggest compliance because of Inuit rules of polite behavior.[30]

Nowdingwah seated in front of musk ox fur (W385)

"The facial characteristics of many individuals in the tribe are noticeably Asiatic. The obliquely set eyes are a common occurrence. The natural aptness for imitations shown by many is also strikingly suggestive of a Chinese and Japanese trait." [Robert E. Peary, Northward over the 'Great Ice': A Narrative of Life and Work Along the Shores and Upon the Interior Ice-Cap of Northern Greenland in the Years 1886 and 1891–1897, Vol I *(New York: Frederick A. Stokes Company, 1898), 487.]*

29.   Rosenblum, *A World History of Photography,* 45–72.
30.   Pamela Stern, "The History of Canadian and Arctic Photography: Issues of Territorial and Cultural Sovereignty," in *Imaging the Arctic,* 50.

Photographing the Inuit tupik [tent] (B263)

" . . . showing the habit of disrobing while in the tupik." (Bement Log)

Inuk boy and his mother (B264)

"Each tent has a raised platform, upon which all sleep. The edge of this makes a seat, and on each side are placed stone lamps in which blubber is burned with moss as a wick. Over this is a drying rack, also a few sticks, but there is no other furniture." [Frederick Albert Cook, My Attainment of the Pole: Being the Record of the Expedition That First Reached the Boreal Center, 1907–1909. (New York: The Polar Publishing Company, 1911), 49]

Wyckoff, Bement, and the other guests of the *Erik* were enthusiasts, yet they were not professional photographers. They used good quality equipment—by 1901 standards—and they worked together to achieve provocative photographic images. Through their lenses, we see life aboard ship, we see the Inuit lifestyle, but also remarkably, we catch a glimpse of the way men thought at the turn of the century.

Perspectives on Race

Social norms in 1901 were quite different than they are today. According to historian Dana Takagi, "until the early twentieth century, white people thought that biological distinctions among groups explained differences in character and culture. Correspondingly, the practice of ranking people by race and subordinating groups . . . was viewed as a natural and justifiable consequence of the biological superiority of whites."[31]

The American public undoubtedly considered Matthew Henson inferior to his white counterparts in the early 1900s. An African American who worked alongside Peary on numerous polar expeditions, Henson became fluent in the Inuit language, understood their culture, and even lived with the Inuit. His ability and expertise played an important role in Robert Peary's success. However, because of his skin color and the American public's feeling about race, decades elapsed before Henson received any of the recognition he deserved for his contribution to Arctic history.

Some scholars believe Robert Peary was progressive and chose Henson to accompany him on his expeditions because he valued Henson's ability, and others believe he chose him in part because he was black and would not receive equal status as a discoverer of the North Pole. Perhaps both are true. In his 1898 book, *Northward over the 'Great Ice'*, Peary refers to Henson as "my faithful coloured boy . . . the equal of others in the party"[32] and to the Inuit as "my uncontaminated, pure-blooded,

31. Dana Takagi. "Racial Discrimination," in *Reader's Companion to U.S. Women's History*, ed. Wilma Mankiller, et. al. (Boston: Houghton Mifflin Company, 1998), 491–93.
32. Robert E. Peary, *Northward over the 'Great Ice': A Narrative of Life and Work Along the Northern Shores and Upon the Interior Ice-Cap of Northern Greenland in the Years 1886 and 1891–1897* (New York: Frederick A. Stokes Company, 1898), 1: 424.

Matthew Henson in front of musk ox fur backdrop (B353/WII)

"In the context of the time, their relationship was as close to a friendship as one could imagine between a white boss and a black assistant. In Henson, Peary had found an experienced, multitalented aide willing to travel anywhere in support of his ventures. In Peary, Henson had found a well-disposed white sponsor, without whom he had no hope of satisfying his own thirst for travel." [S. Allen Counter, North Pole Legacy: Black, White, and Eskimo. *(Amherst: The University of Massachusetts Press, 1991), 53]*

vigorous, faithful little tribe."[33] Since Robert Peary's writing today seems tainted by a century-old societal standard, his views of Henson and the Inuit are left to interpretation.

In the same way, we need to read between the lines of their diaries and photographs to get a true picture of Wyckoff and Bement and their views about race. It appears that Wyckoff and Bement reflect the American white man's view of race in 1901 since they mention Henson and the Inuit in the same breath, as somehow different than everyone else. Henson appears either sleeping with the Inuit, guiding a group of white men in the Inuit style of hunting, or getting picked up at an Inuit settlement. References to Inuit as "Huskies" and the men's descriptions of their odor, appearance, and lifestyle, although considered insensitive and extremely offensive by today's standards, seem to reflect the typical American view of the time as well. In addition, Wyckoff and Bement seem utterly bewildered by their discovery that three white men, Dr. Dedrick, Robert Stein, and William Warmbath look as dirty as the Inuit and seem comfortable with their Inuit lifestyle.

In some instances, however, Wyckoff and Bement appear to contradict the prevailing attitude about race. In their trading with the people of Godhavn, a village on Disko Island, Louis Bement wrote, "As soon as we got out, we were offered all kinds of stuff for our money, and if anybody thinks that these half-civilized people are not sharp in a trade, they are mistaken. They beat a down east Yankee." Yet, ironically, Wyckoff and Bement admitted they forced the market. The actual prices they paid for such items as handmade sealskin jackets ($1.50) and handmade bearskin pants ($1.50) or a kayak ($1.00) were steals even by 1901 standards.

It could be argued that the Wyckoff and Bement photographs of Matthew Henson resemble photographs taken of white members of the expedition. However, the vast majority of images of Inuit show how dissimilar these people were, which indicates Wyckoff and Bement operated at least in part through their own filter of privilege.

Nevertheless, an understanding and respect for the Inuit resonates from their writing. Wyckoff recognized the difference in the Inuit standard of cleanliness when

33.   Ibid., 508.

he wrote, "It was rather difficult to realize it, but these people have absolutely nothing to live with and on except the animals they kill, the stones they make their huts of, and ice and snow, with a few grasses and mosses that one finds on the coast. As far as I could see, there was absolutely no vegetation at all at this point. There are no conveniences here and one should not blame them perhaps for their filthy conditions, nevertheless mine for the rigging." In another entry, Wyckoff mentioned his irritation with Herbert Berri for taking along too much equipment on their deer[34] hunt, and then making his Inuit guide carry it. Louis Bement's attempt to communicate with the people resulted in a four-page section in his diary in which he recorded common Inuit words and their translations into English.

In discussing Western views of native peoples as seen in mid- to late-nineteenth century photography, the art historian, Naomi Rosenblum, writes, "whether they reinforced dominant stereotypes against nonwhites or made viewers more conscious of individual differences among subjected peoples depended in part on the individual photographer's attitude and approach and in part on the context in which they were seen."[35] Dr. Cook, who was as much an ethnologist as he was a physician, and whom Wyckoff and Bement greatly admired, may have influenced the men in their views of the native people. Dr. Cook conducted Inuit ethnographic studies during his first expedition to the Arctic in 1891. He also learned to speak the Inuit language. In 1902 he wrote:

These northernmost people, almost inhuman in their manner of living, are still, in their relation to each other and to the rest of mankind, very human. They have a deep sense of honor, a wholesome regard for the rights of their fellows, and a sympathetic temperament. Thefts are almost unknown, cheating and lying are extremely uncommon. Quarrels, though frequent, are restrained because of a well-developed habit of suppressing all emotions. Morally, even when measured by our own standard, they are superior to the white invaders of their own country.[36]

Koko (W384/B315)

"Generosity and hospitality are characteristic. There is no such thing up North as individual poverty and riches. It is an unwritten law that when one man has been particularly fortunate in a hunting expedition, his tribe will share the net results. It is this feeling of good fellowship which preserves the race." [Robert Peary, Nearest the Pole: A Narrative of the Polar Expedition of the Peary Arctic Club in the S. S. Roosevelt, *1905-1906. (London: Hutchinson & Company), 385]*

34. Throughout their diaries, Wyckoff and Bement mistakenly refer to caribou as *deer* or *reindeer*. Though members of the same species, their appearance and characteristics are different.
35. Rosenblum, *A World History of Photography*, 170–72.
36. Dr. Frederick Cook, "The People of the Farthest North," *Everybody's Magazine* 6 (1902): 32.

Wyckoff and Bement describe times when they were steered clear of near disasters thanks to the ability and talent of their Inuit hosts. On one occasion, the *Erik* overshot Etah by more than twenty miles. Bement wrote, "When our Eskimo, Kiota came on deck he recognized the country and was very much excited; said we were all dumb, so we turned back." On another occasion Wyckoff wrote, "Church and I were out in the boat with a Husky crew, [and the captain] came so near running us down that we could have touched the boat as she went by us. If the Huskies had not fended off with their oars and backed water we could have had at least a serious accident." So, although Wyckoff and Bement confirm the popular early twentieth century thinking about other races as vastly different, they also show a genuine respect for them personally and for their differences.

The *Erik* Locates the *Windward*

On August 4, 1901, with the help of the Inuit, the *Erik* reached the *Windward* carrying Robert Peary and his wife and daughter. Upon their arrival, the *Erik* party delivered a letter to Robert Peary notifying him of the death of his mother. According to several accounts, Peary showed no outward sign of emotion.[37]

The Arctic historian, Andrew Freeman, wrote, "The Pearys greeted the *Erik* party with restrained cordiality."[38] Not understanding the reason for it, Wyckoff grumbled in his diary, "Met them and that's all . . . we got no news; nor have we any at midnight. All is very secret. . . . Think it is damn rotten that I was left out of everything." Later, in his diary, he wrote that Robert Peary "has talked as if we knew (from Bridgman) of his winter work and has made no secret of it whatever." In this excerpt, Wyckoff may have referred to the news of Robert Peary's fathering a child with an Inuk woman.

---

37. Wally Herbert, *The Noose of Laurels: Robert E. Peary and the Race to the North Pole* (New York: Atheneum, 1989), 140.
38. Freeman, *The Case for Doctor Cook,* 70.

The *Windward* crew on the bow of the ship (W28/B90)

Robert Peary with musk ox fur backdrop (B46/W114)

"The first impression was of an iron man, wrecked in ambition, wrecked in physique, wrecked in hope." [Wally Herbert, The Noose of Laurels: Robert E. Peary and the Race to the North Pole. *(New York: Atheneum, 1989), 139]*

Peary Family at Red Cliff, McCormick Bay (B108/W23)

Site of house they shared beginning in the summer of 1891.

Wyckoff and Bement learned that Robert Peary spent the winter at Fort Conger, over 200 miles away from his wife and daughter who were stranded at Cape Sabine, on the *Windward*.[39] During this time, Josephine Peary discovered her husband's infidelity while talking to an Inuk woman, Allikasingwah. Unaware of the difference in mores, Allikasingwah openly spoke of her relationship with Robert Peary. According to historian John Edward Weems "Jo Peary was stunned by the revelation." She wrote to her husband, "You will have been surprised, perhaps annoyed, when you hear that I came up on a ship . . . but believe me had I known how things were with you here I should not have come."[40]

Though initially troubled by her husband's infidelity, Josephine Peary stood by Robert Peary and by the time of the arrival of the *Erik,* she seemed more concerned about his health than about anything else. At her urging, and the urging of Herbert Bridgman, Peary permitted Dr. Cook to examine him.[41] In his unpublished autobiography written in the 1930s, Dr. Cook recalled that he conducted a thorough examination of Peary when Peary and Mrs. Peary asked him to do so independently. Dr. Cook entered the following in Robert Peary's case file:

> Peary was six feet four inches, age forty-nine years, weight under normal, muscular development uneven. The arm and chest muscles were good, but the legs were thin. The feet were crippled by old ulcers, the result of repeated frostbites [*sic*]. Eight of his toes had been removed leaving painful stubs which refused to heal. In the face there was an absence of normal expression, a vacant stare from the eyes, a morbid cherry brown in the skin of the face. The skin of the body was pale, hard in texture and hung in baggy folds. It's [*sic*] color was gruesome—not brown like the face—but grey green with just a little submerged yellow. All outward appearances were those of one affected with some morbid disease.[42]

---

39.   Ibid., 68.

40.   John Edward Weems, *Peary: The Explorer and the Man* (London: Eyre & Spottiswoode, 1967), 190.

41.   Freeman, *The Case for Doctor Cook,* 70.

42.   Frederick A. Cook. "Hell is a Cold Place" (Frederick A. Cook Papers, Manuscript Division, Library of Congress, Washington, D.C.).

Dr. Cook made a diagnosis of pernicious anemia. He recommended that Peary eat a diet of raw meat and he suggested that he return home with the *Erik* for a period of recovery. Peary refused to follow either suggestion. Dr. Cook recalled that "Since Peary in this sad plight would not be guided by the advice of his wife or his physician, nor by the suggestions of his friends on the ship, who had his best interests at heart, all determined to co-operate with the leader's determination to make the best of a seemingly impossible situation."[43] A month later, in a *New York Times* statement, Herbert Bridgman silenced any public uncertainty over Peary's physical condition when he said, "During the entire two years since he has been heard from, his health has been excellent, and the accident to his feet at Fort Conger in 1899 has caused him but slight inconvenience and has in no way impaired his efficiency in the field."[44]

Hunting in 1901

When it became clear that Robert Peary would be staying in the Arctic rather than returning on the *Erik*, Wyckoff and Bement learned that a large part of their responsibility involved hunting and preserving meat for the following year. Determined to make another dash for the pole, Mr. Peary needed food for his dogs, and food for the many men and women who would help him. In his notes, several years later, Bement recalled that:

> Walrus hunting next to the Rhino and African Buffalo is the most thrilling hunting to be had. You are out in a whaleboat among the ice pans and if you happen to get into a herd of from 50 to a 100 of them, they surround the boat and try to puncture it with their tusks or get the tusks over the gunwale and you are shooting at them as fast you can load. The Eskimos [are] hitting them with the oars and I can vouch that goose pimples as large as

43. Ibid.
44. *New York Times,* 14 September 1901.

**Bement (center) and Stone hunting from
aft deck** (W92)

*"Peary decided to make another dash in 1902 and [it was]
up to us to get supplies. Walrus, reindeer, seals, polar bear,
musk oxen, and duck of all kinds. This country simply
vomits with game." (Bement Notes)*

Professor Limond Stone with a pair of ivory gulls (W34)

" . . . everything they have comes of an animal: food, clothing, kayaks (boats) sledges, harpoons, lines." (Bement Notes)

hickory nuts stand out on you to say nothing of one's hair standing. They weigh from one to two tons each and [they are] wonderfully swift and graceful swimmers. [They] would tow a whaleboat when harpooned with eight men in it so that water would come aboard. [It was] some experience for a layman but we got used to it after several hunts [and we] never lost the thrills.[45]

While it is true that around the turn of the century affluent visitors from Western countries visited exotic places in order to search for prized game trophies, the guests of the *Erik* hunted expressly to provide Peary with provisions for his upcoming year of exploration.

Forrest Wood, Jr., in his book, *The Delights and Dilemmas of Hunting: The Hunting Versus Anti-Hunting Debate,* stresses the importance of distinguishing between different types of hunting.[46] Commercial hunting by frontier businessmen differed enormously from the kind of subsistence hunting practiced by the Inuit and Robert Peary. Though they may have killed an alarming number of animals on the *Erik,* and no doubt, it was thrilling, the men worked with the Inuit to learn their style of hunting. Unlike commercial operations that killed exponentially higher numbers and abandoned what they could not sell, the Inuit killed what they needed and used every bit of the animal.

Dr. Thomas Dedrick

Wyckoff and Bement learned firsthand about Robert Peary's work through their efforts to resolve a dispute between Peary and his former physician, Dr. Thomas Dedrick. As Wyckoff and Bement related in their diaries, Robert Peary and Dr. Dedrick became embroiled in a clash around the time of the arrival of the *Erik.* Dr. Dedrick resigned his position with Mr. Peary and refused to accept Peary's demand

45. Personal notes, private collection, Ayer family.
46. Forrest Wood, Jr. *The Delights and Dilemmas of Hunting: The Hunting versus Anti-Hunting Debate* (Lanham, Maryland: University Press of America, 1997), 16.

that he return home on the *Erik*. Dr. Dedrick also resigned from the *Peary Arctic Club*. In newspaper reports of the time, the second engineer of the *Erik* was quoted as saying, "owing to a misunderstanding with Mr. Peary, Dr. Dedrick, of Brooklyn, who had been with Mr. Peary during the last five years, was left behind at Etah, and it was understood that he was not to be brought home on any ship belonging to the Arctic Club."[47] Numerous newspaper reports declared that Dr. Dedrick resigned as doctor of the expedition either because he was mentally unsound, or because he was angry that Peary did not choose him to command the expedition in his absence. One article even stated that he resigned because he wanted to make a dash for the pole on his own.[48]

Though Dr. Dedrick never made public the exact reason for his resignation from the *Peary Arctic Club,* several reports stated his reason for remaining in the North was his distress over an epidemic occurring within the Inuit community. Many of Dr. Dedrick's Inuit friends contracted a fatal illness acquired from the explorers either personally or through food. As their physician, Dr. Dedrick felt a responsibility to provide them with medical treatment. In a newspaper report at the time, his brother, Henry C. Dedrick, of Washington, New Jersey, said, "It is not surprising that differences have arisen. It would be absurd to suppose that two high-strung men could be in each other's company for three years in the frozen North, subjected to the terrific mental and physical strain, without controversies arising."[49]

Dr. Dedrick's refusal to return on the *Erik,* and Dr. Cook's involvement in resolving the dispute, as chronicled in the Wyckoff-Bement diaries, profoundly affected Wyckoff and Bement, and helped them form lasting impressions of Dr. Cook and Robert Peary when they later became controversial Arctic figures. In preparing notes for a lecture he gave several decades after the expedition, Louis Bement wrote of the Peary-Cook controversy:

Dr. Thomas Dedrick (W16/B95)
"The reason I remained in the Arctic was purely one of duty to the expedition, and was not for any monetary purpose." (Dr. Dedrick in New York Times, *22 September 1902)*

47.   *Evening Telegram,* New York City, 21 September 1901.
48.   *New York Times,* 22 September 1902.
49.   *Newark Sunday News,* 5 April 1959.

Afternoon on the *Erik* (W96)

Henson (front left), Peary (at wheel), Cook (standing in center, wearing Inuk men's sealskin parka) and two Inuit (right).

We had the opportunity to study both of these men in the field and we had great admiration for them. Neither was any novice in Arctic work. And when you are shaking hands with accidents and possible death every hour in a country known as 'No mans land,' where the law of God is forgotten and the law of man does not reach, where that 'veil of civilization' is torn off from you, where every bit of meanness comes to the surface from selfness, fear, and you the individual stand naked among your fellow man, there is the spot and the only spot where there is an absolute record of yourself. Then you can judge man and it was here we judged each other.[50]

Bement in full Arctic attire (W62)

50.   Personal notes, private collection, Ayer family.

DIARIES

Louis C. Bement

(B352/W6)

Clarence F. Wyckoff

(B350/W10)

N.B.: Un-bracketed italicized sections were in original but were left out of rewritten version

SATURDAY, JULY 6TH, 1901

Left for New York. Took sail down the lake with the people. Left me at Renwick pier.[51] *Never hated to leave as much as did this time. Guess it was because all the women were waving handkerchiefs and things and it embarrassed me to walk down the pier; kind of upset me. Don't care for expression, "Goodbye, hope I'll see you again," nor the expression of face, which goes with it.*

—Wyckoff

SUNDAY, JULY 7TH, 1901

Left Ithaca at 9:20 P.M. [Took the] D. L. & W.[52] [train] for New York City. *Hard to leave Belle and the kids. Mother surprised me by keeping up.*[53] Every one of the family down in the mouth, never expecting to see me again. All kept their nerve except little Lucie who broke down, begged me not to go. Dr. Howe took me to the train, said last farewells at depot. They illuminated the house so that I saw it from the train on the hill. I felt rather sad and turned in at 10 P.M.

—Bement

Met Church[54] *in New York.*

M. Richard-Paris; model 1900 Zeiss lenses, Veriscope (2 magazines), leather box, stereoscopic machine, al. tripod, Gimmneau plates (extra rapid and extra thin),

ground glass attachment, plates keep several years, lactate silver plates for positives.

—Wyckoff

MONDAY, JULY 8TH, 1901

Arrived in New York at 6:30 A.M. *Slept very little on train; too much thought of home.* Went directly to Hoffman House. Found C. F. Wyckoff and A. W. Church. Took breakfast in our rooms. Then started out purchasing supplies for trip. Spent entire day so doing except part of the afternoon to see Mr. H. L. Bridgman at The Standard Union office, Brooklyn, the commander of the expedition, who gave us a number of pointers: what to get, also just what our capacity on the trip should be i.e., guests of the club[55] and wholly under his orders in every way.

—Bement

Louis arrived. Also Brick and Alp.[56] *Hottest day I ever experienced. Bought snowshoes, felt boots and outfit. Saw Bridgman and arranged route to North Sydney [Nova Scotia].*

—Wyckoff

TUESDAY, JULY 9TH, 1901

Took cab to see Metcalf and Kinney off for a trip to Norway. Spent rest of morning buying more things for the outfit; nothing too much or [too]

---

51. Located in Renwick Park, which is now Stewart Park, on Lake Cayuga, Ithaca, New York. In 1901, the Cayuga Lake Railway Company terminated at Renwick Park.
52. Delaware, Lackawanna and Western.
53. Probably referring to his wife's keeping the kids up late to say goodbye.
54. Alfred Church met Wyckoff through the Chi Psi Fraternity at Cornell University. He also was a friend of Bement.
55. *Peary Arctic Club.*
56. William Metcalf Jr. and John Alpin Kinney were friends of Wyckoff through the Chi Psi Fraternity at Cornell University. They also became friends of Bement.

good. We are going to have fine outfit. Afternoon was spent in packing trunks, boxes and traveling bags: 5 trunks, 4 pack bags, 3 boxes. At night Delahunty gave us a farewell dinner at Shanley's[57] (fine); then took in the theater. Turned in at 1 P.M.
—Bement

Saw Brick and Alp off to Norway.
—Wyckoff

WEDNESDAY, JULY 10TH, 1901
Up at 6 A.M. Breakfast in rooms. Cab at 7 A.M. for Central Station. Took train at 8 A.M. for Boston. Arrived there at 2:30 P.M. Cab for S.[S.] Prince George, for Yarmouth, Nova Scotia. Sailed at 4 P.M. Wyckoff had hard time in getting the baggage over on time and checked. Boston Harbor is grand. I had a slight touch of seasickness, just enough to miss an elegant supper.
—Bement

Today we started on our trip. Church and Bement have been here two or three days, and we have been purchasing outfit and supplies. Monday was, I think the hottest day I ever experienced. Bought snow shoes, felt boots, etc.

We called Mr. Bridgman to inquire as to what provisions, etc., it was advisable to take along, but he assured us that it was not necessary for us to take anything, as he had arranged for plenty of everything.

We have with us twelve pieces of baggage, and on arrival in Boston it was a rush to get them all aboard the boat, as we had but an hour's time for the transfer. Sunset 7:10 P.M.
—Wyckoff

THURSDAY, JULY 11TH, 1901
Arrived at Yarmouth at 8:15 A.M. Fine trip from Boston. Heavy fog this A.M. Passed the Customs officials with our luggage and a ten-dollar bill. All okay. Got it sealed through. The fog whistle was busy all night so did not get much sleep. The ship lost her bearings; picked up St. Johns buoy and got bearings, all okay, so we made train. I shaved on board Wednesday and [in] so doing, Lucie's wished-on ring came off.[58] Made impression on my mind; cannot get over it.

Distance traveled so far:

Ithaca to New York	261
New York to Boston	226
Boston to Yarmouth	250

Everything going fine. Nothing too good in the eat, sleep and smoking line for us. We are traveling like kings. *Arrived at Yarmouth at 8:15 A.M.* Sun set at 7:50 P.M. Days getting longer. Left Yarmouth at 9:30 A.M. Nothing much to see in the town. Fine train and service. Arrived in Halifax at 4:30 P.M.
—Bement

---

57. A restaurant on West 43rd Street in New York City.

58. His seven-year-old daughter made a wish on his ring for good luck, and the ring may have fallen off.

Clarence Wyckoff on deck in his
slippers (W32/B92)

Arrived Yarmouth and Halifax. Halifax bum town like Kingston and most Canuck towns. Bum hotel, bum everything. Got more supplies, 6 boxes.
—Wyckoff

FRIDAY, JULY 12TH, 1901
Took a hack ride through Halifax. Strange old town, old buildings, etc. Fine fortifications and harbor. Stopped at the Queens Hotel; slept in a trundle bed. Went down to Captain Farquhar's office. Found he had gone to Sydney. Bought canned goods for the trip. Wyckoff got $100.00 draft cashed at bank. No trouble about identification. Left at 12 noon for North Sydney on the fast express. Fine train and service. Very fast. Arrived at Mulgrave at 8 P.M., eastern point of Nova Scotia, where we ferry over to Cape Breton Island. Passengers get off the train on the boat; cars run on a big barge boat warped along side and over the straits. Two miles very interesting, but great loss of time and expense to RR Company. Nova Scotia looks like a good grazing country. Everything looks stunted, especially the trees, however, they say there is large timber inland. Saw the Bay of Fundy, 52-foot tides, rivers as large as Cayuga Lake[59] empty and fill every 12 hours.

Arrived at North Sydney at 11:30 P.M. Found a carry-all [wagon] at depot; all got in and took as rough and wild [a] ride as I ever care to. They forgot the springs on the wagon. Also, to turn out for the stones. Stopped at the Vendome Hotel,

inquired for Dr. Cook; [he] was out. We went into the side room to get some ginger ale and sat there talking over our trip when Dr. Cook appeared. The celebrated Antarctic and Arctic explorer, surgeon, and second in command to the expedition. We found him a most interesting man. He had been here for two days getting supplies, sailors, and making final arrangements for the trip. Berri and Stone with Berri's father and mother were here stopping over to Sydney across the bay. We went down and looked over the ship [the *Erik*]. Was so dark could not see much. Returned to [the] hotel and turned in. Hard, tough-looking inn with a tough-looking gang hanging around. Wyckoff would not lock the door. I hid my money; his scattered over the room.
—Bement

Arrived at Sidney via a train from Halifax. *Train hour and half late. Every train and boat we have taken has been over an hour late.* Left Boston by boat to Yarmouth, and went from Yarmouth to Halifax by train. Halifax is like all Canadian towns, slow and dead. Hotel conditions rank. We purchased a small lot of supplies, simply extras, as olives, sardines, pickles, etc.
—Wyckoff

SATURDAY, JULY 13TH, 1901
Up at 7 A.M. Met Captain James Farquhar, owner of the Erik, jolly old salt. Kept everybody in a roar

59. Over sixty miles long, Cayuga is the largest of the Finger Lakes of upstate New York.

Train from Halifax to North Sydney (C20B)

Dr. Cook (left) and Bement on a carry-all (C20A)

of laughter in the dining room. Down to the Erik after breakfast. Took a dozen snapshots at her and mailed them home. Met Captain Blakeney, First Mate Bartlett, the ice navigator, a character. Looks like McTodd,[60] the character in Pearson's magazine.[61] Took my last shave and bath. Would not [have] shaved but expect to take dinner with Berri today. Mr. Bridgman arrived at 10:30 A.M. Expected to sail at noon but his trunk with all the charts did not come, so held up till midnight; then we will be off. North Sydney is like all Canadian towns built on a side hill and old-fashioned. We have been buying more supplies in shape of fruits. Bought the town out of cabbage, potatoes, peaches, bananas, etc.
—Bement

Went on board the Erik. It is a good boat, barkentine rig[62] auxiliary propeller, makes about seven and one-half miles an hour in favorable weather. Met Dr. Cook, Stone, and Berri. Bridgman arrived late. Officers on ship: Captain Blakeney, First Officer Moses Bartlett, [and] Second Officer Will Bartlett. Both Bartletts are from New Foundland and look like a good pair. Chief Engineer: Fullerton. Met Mr. and Mrs. Berri, Mr. and Mrs. Price. Are here to see Berri and Stone off. Met Mr. Hoppin, a crazy millionaire.[63] Is crazy on the subject of "Down North." *Gave everybody matches (small boxes)* and was always in a great hurry. "How are you? Good-bye"

was his usual salutation. He was with Peary on one of his trips and has always shown great interest in every polar expedition. Wrote a crazy book on his trip. Although the weather was warm he wore a heavy overcoat and muffler about his neck as if he still thought he was in the Arctic region. *Sun set at 8:00 P.M.*
—Wyckoff

SUNDAY, JULY 14TH, 1901

Got Mr. Bridgman's trunk down at 11:30 last night and the post office opened the mail for us. Received a letter from Belle [Mrs. Bement]; first one since leaving home but still we did not get away as expected. Short of sailors and a cook. Our cook deserted. It is getting discouraging. Everybody has the blues. Slept aboard last night. Berth a thin, very thin, mattress laid over boards. If I have to endure this for two or three months, possibly a year, I can put up with any old thing in the sleeping line. Suppose I have lots before me. We have come across the most accommodating people in Nova Scotia and Cape Breton Island one could imagine. They are doing everything for us, except to find sailors and a cook. They (sailors) are the greatest cowards I ever came in contact with. We are offering extra money, but when the captain tells them where our destination is, they cannot get up the companionway fast enough.

---

60. A fictional character in a series of short stories by Cutliffe Hyne, McTodd was a hard-drinking Scottish engineer who traveled around the world, including among Inuit.

61. A popular general interest magazine, it was begun in Britain and brought to the United States in 1899.

62. A barkentine rig has three or more masts, square-rigged on the foremast and fore-and-aft-rigged on the other masts.

63. Benjamin Hoppin was on the 1896 Peary Arctic Expedition and published a diary about it.

Erik at North Sydney, Cape Breton Island, Nova Scotia (B131)

"Capt. Grey, master of the Erik for more than fifteen years, says that she is a very fine seagoing ship, and does good work in the ice." (Confidential Report to the Members of the Peary Arctic Club, 12 June 1902, [E])

Chief Engineer Fullerton (W20)

Our party consists of:

H. L. Bridgman	COMMANDER
Dr. Frederick A. Cook	2ND COMMANDER
C. F. Wyckoff	Ithaca, New York
A. W. Church	Elgin, Ill.
Herbert Berri	Brooklyn, N.Y.
L. C. Stone	Brooklyn, N.Y.
L.C. Bement	Ithaca, N.Y.

Crew:

J. U. Blakeney	
CAPTAIN	Dartmouth, Nova Scotia
Moses Bartlett	
1ST MATE	Brigus, Newfoundland
William Bartlett	
2ND MATE	Brigus, Newfoundland
Fullerton	
CHIEF ENGINEER	Halifax, Nova Scotia
Stauts	
2ND ENGINEER	

6 Sailors

4 Firemen

2 Oilers

1 Cook

1 Steward

Have been unpacking our goods and arranging them all day. Wyckoff and I occupy one cabin. Church has one all to himself. We put up 2 dozen hooks and one cannot see the walls for the stuff hung up. We are still short 3 sailors and a cook. If we can only get a cook, will sail. And the captain [Blakeney] says that he will work and sign us as A.B. seamen[64] as they would not permit us to sail short-handed. A cook at last. Goodbyes at 11:20 A.M. All aboard, lines cast off at 11:50 A.M. All hustle and bustle, whistles blowing, flags dipped[65] from all the ships in the harbor. Great send off. We are all doing something. Wyckoff and I at the wheel. Berri, Stone, Cook, and Bridgman doing ordinary sailor work. Very warm.

Arrived at Cape North at 8 P.M. Wyckoff, Church, Berri, and second mate gone ashore for sailors; no success. Anchor up at 11 P.M. for Newfoundland. Everybody feeling fine and glad to get away. Tried cod fishing at Cape North. No success, as usual. A storm coming up. Lots of lightning and a phosphorus sea.

—Bement

---

64. Able-bodied seamen are members of the deck department of a merchant vessel.

65. Lowered and then raised.

Inspecting the *Erik* with Dr. Cook before departure (C17A)

*"As a matter of fact, I imagine the captain [Farquhar, the owner of the Erik]
was rather a busy man. When we arrived at North Sydney, he seemed quite
anxious that we should get under way, and did everything in his power to assist
us in getting an early start." (Wyckoff Notes)*

Waving goodbye to the *Erik* (W182/B349)
The pier at North Sydney, Nova Scotia.

Sailed at 11:50 A.M. Expected to leave last night, but were minus a cook. He deserted the ship. If he is caught he will get six months in prison. The sailors get part of their pay in advance and then skip out and look up a new job. It was necessary for us to keep a constant watch on the men for fear they would desert in this way. The first mate was drunk when we started and so were most of the sailors.

We got a cook this morning, a nineteen-year-old boy who had been a tailor's apprentice and ran away to sea. He has never seen a stove before as far as I can make out. We are short-handed for a crew, have only three sailors, need six. Found out later that we should have had ten or twelve sailors.

This afternoon I rowed ashore three miles, with Church and Will Bartlett to see if we could get men at Aspee Bay, Cape Breton. Were unsuccessful. *Foliage small.*
—Wyckoff

MONDAY, JULY 15TH, 1901
At 2 A.M. very foggy and rough. Lost bearings. Struck a port twelve miles from destination, which is Porte aux Basque. In port at 5 P.M. Went ashore to telegraph office and post office. Took pictures. Stone, Dr. [Cook], Berri, and I took supper ashore. Nothing but rocks, rocks [*sic*], sod houses, and fishing boats. Curious people. Telegraphed for sailors at St. Johns. Got reply that three are on the way.
—Bement

Arrived Port aux Basque, New Foundland; still looking for men. Telegraphed to St. Johns and arranged for three, but they won't arrive until the 17th. Everybody seems to have heard ghost stories of "Down North" and are [*sic*] afraid to tackle the job.

Get book by woman "Down North & Up Along" published by Rogers Brothers, Boston, 1900. Send books to William Raymond MacKay, Port-aux-Basque: Deliverance Island, Jules Verne & Company.

Have hives all over, much and yet again. Had to go on deck at night to cool off. New Foundland fine hilly country, no timber near the coast, small timber inland. Caribou in quantity; also salmon. No preserves.[66] Railroad from Port-aux-Basque to St. Johns, five hundred and forty-seven miles. *Go to Bay of Islands to outfit for caribou.*
—Wyckoff

TUESDAY, JULY 16TH, 1901
Aboard all day developing pictures. Nothing doing.
—Bement

Spent the day wandering over the town taking photos and seeing the sights. New Foundlander kids are very bright. They have no horses here, as they can raise no feed. *Had a bath on deck after dark.*
—Wyckoff

66. For maintaining and reserving fish or game for private hunting or fishing.

Port aux Basques, Newfoundland (W187)

*l. to r. Stone, young boy, Dr. Cook, and Berri. "We discovered first that
we had but 3 sailors where we should have had 12, and this necessitated
our laying over for 3 days in Newfoundland while we could augment our
crew." (Wyckoff Notes)*

WEDNESDAY JULY 17TH, 1901

Ashore in morning with Bridgman. Got some supplies aboard at 12 P.M. Slept on deck three hours. Church and Wyckoff [went] brook trout fishing. Berri, Stone, Dr. [Cook], and I went to a Church of England supper. Took the phonograph; astonished the natives. Aboard at 9 P.M. The three sailors arrived. Anchor up [at] 9:35 P.M. Laid to[67] until 11:20 P.M. waiting for a pilot. Now we are off for the north in earnest and all hands delighted. Had enough disappointments. The night is dark and the channel [is] very narrow. The captain does not like the job of going out tonight but Mr. Bridgman said yes, so out we go. Wrote my last letter to Belle[68] today unless we stop on the Labrador which Mr. Bridgman says [it is] not [possible to do]. Caught codfish and sea bass today. Fine eating.
—Bement

Went after trout with Church. Caught fourteen small ones right near town, and the pond was all fished out. Must be good fishing further inland.
   Sailed *for* "Down North" with full crew 10:45 P.M. *Fine night. No one seasick yet.*
—Wyckoff

THURSDAY, JULY 18TH, 1901

Up at 8 A.M. Everybody spent morning taking pictures. Have been promoted from doing sailor work to assisting the captain taking observations. Slept part of the afternoon. We are off shore from eight to ten miles. The Newfoundland coast is very rocky and bold, rising from 200' to 1500' high. Very picturesque. Weather fine. Up in the crow's nest today. We caught the cabin boy stealing our cigars today. Captain [Blakeney] says a very remarkable trip so far on account of the fine clear weather and smooth sea. Everybody having the finest of times and glad we came. Brook trout for dinner [was] fine. The coast [of Newfoundland] is lined with hundreds of little islands.
—Bement

Gulf of St. Lawrence
—Wyckoff

FRIDAY, JULY 19TH, 1901

Wet, cloudy, raining, sea smooth. Sighted coast of Labrador at 8 A.M. Set sails this morning for the first time. Few fishing boats in sight; on look out for whales. Sighted a whale, as I supposed, and got all hands on the bridge; it turned out to be a small boat. I got a thumping from all hands. I promised I would never sight another whale. We saw our first iceberg this noon off the Labrador coast. Others coming in sight through Belle Isle Straits. Coast of Labrador low and high lands, back topped off with snow.
   Took photos of two large bergs. At 5 P.M. there are 55 medium and large bergs in sight and one immense fellow; any quantity of flow and pan ice. Thermometer at 2 P.M. [is] 48½°F, [a] drop of

---

67. To lie relatively stationary, usually with the head of the ship as near the wind as possible.

68. Louis Bement's wife was Addie Belle Bement.

Domino Run, Labrador (B27)

Louis Bement (left) and Dr. Cook pose for the camera
(W121/B75)

A leisurely day on the deck (W88B)

Berri hangs from the rigging while Dr. Cook takes photograph.

Icebergs (W263/B234)

"Greenland is entirely covered with ice from a [sic] 100' to 9000 feet thick except for a ribbon on the coast from a few feet to a few miles to this inland ice." (Bement Notes)

First Mate, Moses Bartlett, of *Erik* (W60)

"He was wildly drunk and he was cursing the captain in two or three languages. I do not mean to insinuate that the mate was an educated man, as his knowledge of languages extended only through the cursing department." (Wyckoff Notes)

The icebergs loom larger (W312)

nearly 10 degrees since noon. All putting on extra outer clothing. Thermometer at 5 P.M., 44°F, and falling. We are into the ice pans and bergs. Great sight to watch the ship plow through them and push them aside. Could not see a drop of open water at 6 P.M. Great deal of faultfinding by [the] first mate [Moses Bartlett] because the captain [Blakeney] does not go into them at full speed. Turned in at 10 P.M. We have stopped at 11 P.M. The captain is ramming the ice; sounds in the berth as if we were going into a gravel bed. At 2 A.M. we stop; can not go ahead or stern; completely hemmed in by pan ice.[69] We are now in Belle Isle Strait, laid to till 4 A.M. Anchored to a large pan. Started again but in the dense fog and rain we ran into an extra thick pan which brought the ship to a standstill. It broke off a large piece, which went bumping under the keel, and when it struck the rudder, it raised the ship up several feet, and threw the man at the wheel completely over it into the scuppers[70] on [the] other side. Our first hard bump and it made us all a little nervous and taught us a lesson [about] how to manage the wheel in the ice. Held up again for an hour. Then ahead at 1/4 speed but bump, bump, bump; impossible to sleep. We sighted open water and hoped we were on the outside of the pack. Disappointed again for more ice in sight and it looks heavier. But I suppose disappointments are half the pleasures of Arctic navigation.
—Bement

We have crossed the Gulf of New Foundland with nothing of special interest happening. The shores of New Foundland are about the same here as at Port aux Basque. We are now in the Straits of Belle Isle and have seen our first icebergs. At one time I counted fifty-seven all in sight at once. They appear to me to be much higher than they really are. I made a bet—*a quart of wine*—with Dr. Cook that one was one hundred feet high, and lost. It was only sixty to eighty feet by the captain's sextant. Have passed higher and larger bergs since. Toward night we ran into much pan ice, or as the New Foundlanders call them "growlers." Have seen a couple of seal, many ducks, [and] *two* loons. At 11:05 P.M. we are going at lowest speed. Much ice and fog. Every minute the ship gets a jar, the captain, who is opposite me, jumps up. He is absolutely unfamiliar with the ice conditions and is nervous and scared. He has just gone on deck to inspect the ship and tie up to a cake of ice. There is enough ice here to supply the city of New York for a thousand years. Temperature: 44°F. We are above 51° north latitude. It is a grand sight here amidst the ice. Feel more than repaid for my trip so far.
—Wyckoff

SATURDAY, JULY 20TH, 1901
On deck at 8:30 A.M. Foggy and raining. Nothing but ice in sight. No bergs, just pans from 10 feet square to a mile in size. Our occupation today seems to be making cracked ice and we are very

69.   Ice broken from a large floe and floating in open water.
70.   A drain at the edge of a deck exposed to the weather, for allowing accumulated water to drain away into the sea or into the bilges.

successful; however, making but little headway. Sometimes we have to lay to for from one half to two hours. At 6:30 P.M. the captain anchors to a large pan refusing to go on, on account of fog and ice. Two hawsers[71] out from bow, one midship and stern; heavy gale blowing but we feel no motion from the sea. The pans keep it down. It will break up the pack. At 3:30 A.M. we started again.

—Bement

Fog, rain, ice, wind. A good combination to tie to, and we are tied to it for fair [sic]. We have lines out to a big pan waiting for light to find an opening. Have given up the idea of making a Labrador port and will make for Disko direct as soon as we can get loose.

Have played many games of chess with Stone and have won about one third of them. *Knows a [good] deal about game.* The Doctor [Cook] tells tales of the South and North. Peary on icecap; bitten by dogs. Takes whiskey and it made him drunk. Attempted to put feet *into* snow under the sleeping bag.

Verhoeff probably crazy.[72] Would take baths in air hole in ice during the winter. Would have to be rescued or would have frozen. In the Antarctic some of the men, *two officers,* went crazy, and all would have been in another year.

—Wyckoff

SUNDAY, JULY 21ST, 1901

Very foggy and raining, loose from the pack at 3:30 A.M. Good deal of bumping until 8 A.M., but making some headway. At 8:30 A.M. started at full speed; ice very rotten and easily broken up or pushed aside. Heaviest fog yet [we] don't know our position. Have not had an observation for three days and the log has had to be in on account of the ice, so our position is in doubt. Captain's guess is latitude 53°, longitude 51°. Bridgman and Cook both say that they never saw as much and heavy ice in this section on any of their trips. The intention was to follow the coast of Labrador but the ice has driven us out into the Atlantic hundreds of miles. They do not expect to encounter any heavier, or more, ice off the coast of Greenland. It has been stop and start all night long, but the ice is getting lighter and less every mile.

—Bement

It is lucky I have a daybook or I would not know it was Sunday. All days look alike on the Erik. Sometime during the night we got out of the ice. Our course is now east by north. We are leaving the Labrador coast and starting for Greenland. Our actual course is almost direct north, but we are getting up alongside of the magnetic pole, and hence, the north pole of our needle is pointing around toward the west. We eventually get almost

---

71. A hawser is a large diameter rope used for mooring a ship.
72. John M. Verhoeff was a mineralogist and meteorologist who mysteriously disappeared in the Arctic in 1892 during the expedition of the *S. S. Kite.* See Andrew Freeman, *The Case for Doctor Cook,*

29–30; Frederick A. Cook, "The Disappearance of Verhoeff: An Unsolved Arctic Mystery. (The Frederick A. Cook Society Collection. Byrd Polar Research Center. The Ohio State University, Columbus, Ohio).

A miserable day on the *Erik* (W108)

*"We were crossing Baffin Bay, which the sailors told us was the roughest
piece of water in the world, and I do not believe they lied much at that.
At one time the indicator showed that we dipped 30° each way from the
perpendicular." (Wyckoff Notes)*

due north of the magnetic North Pole, which is somewhere over in Grinnell about 72° north latitude. According to the chart at Etah, the compass is about 110° out of the way. I sat up most of the night on account of hives. Temperature [is] 37°F.
—Wyckoff

MONDAY, JULY 22ND, 1901

Up at 8 A.M. Foggy, raining and generally very nasty. Now on the edge of the pack; will clear it in an hour. No ice in sight at 10 A.M. All sails set for the first time making about 10 knots. A nasty sea coming up. At 2 P.M. Stone and Berri seasick. At 4 P.M. extremely rough ship has about five different and distinct motions. The pitching is something awful. Part of the sails taken in. The doctor [Cook], Stone and Berri [are] in their bunks. Nasty all day long. Oilskins[73] in style today.
—Bement

Clear of ice; rough sea; signs of seasickness.
—Wyckoff

TUESDAY, JULY 23RD, 1901

Foggy, raining, and extremely rough. Hard night, little sleep. Had to hang on all night to keep in berth. All our gear on the floor of our stateroom all mixed up; a nasty mess. The sea came in the port and wet things down. Bridgman, Stone, and Berri all passed away. Wyckoff, Church and myself all okay. The ship has a roll of 30°. Impossible to stand

on deck without a good strong hold. Table rack used first time today. Wyckoff, Church, and I are taking our three squares nevertheless. I only smoked once today. Slept nearly all this morning. Had to put in the guard board to keep in the bunk. No observations for 6 days. Our position a matter of guess.
—Bement

Yesterday and today we have been crossing Baffins Bay and it has been exceedingly rough. The sailors all claim that Baffins Bay is always rough and always a very nasty sheet of water. Cook, Bridgman, Berri, and Stone are confined to bed. Very seasick. The captain is a little sick. Claims it is a touch of liver. Louis looks a trifle haggard. Church and I have not been touched. *Very rough.* The ship is rolling 30° each way, away from the perpendicular. We have had on the racks[74] today, but they were useless. Got the soup tureen in my lap—also the soup. Didn't mind tureen or soup, but there were other things. Church, Bement, and myself were the only ones at table. I happened to be serving soup. We have had rice soup now for about seven days straight and I for one was rather tired of it. Perhaps the rough weather had something to do with it, but at any rate, I was not eating, but rather toying with the rice. I noticed it was peculiar rice for it was corrugated, and then I noticed that there were little black dots at one end of each kernel of rice. My curiosity aroused, I examined closer and found that it really

---

73. A waterproof suit of pants and jacket worn by sailors for protection against rain.

74. Referring to table racks designed to hold tableware in place.

was not rice soup at all. The kernels were maggots. I didn't tell the others as I didn't want to spoil their dinner. *Confided my discovery of maggots to Bridgman. Bridgman said we had had them in beef for several days and had kept dark for some reason.* Had a bath! *Very pleasant day.*
—Wyckoff

WEDNESDAY, JULY 24TH, 1901
Up at 8 A.M. Terrible rough night: the worst yet. Everybody up and about deck. First peep of the sun in five days, not very much at that, but we know now that there is such a thing. We are supposed to be opposite the extreme south of Greenland, latitude 60°. In the ice again. Much heavier than we have seen before; also quantities of large bergs. This is the east Greenland ice carried by the current down and around the southern coast, [and] up the west coast. We are sailing more west to avoid it. Saw a seal today; the first one. Church shot one but on account of so much ice, did not get it. We saw a large berg doing its best to turn over. A remarkable sight. The captain gave it a wide berth. I have the hives [and] suffer the torments of hell. Cannot sleep on account of the fever. I have to walk the deck nights in my pajamas to cool off. Clarence has had them three days. They are awful. He is a mass of sores on the legs and I am getting [them] there also. We discovered maggots in the soup. We have been eating them for a day or two. They came from the meat we brought from Sydney. I thought they were rice or barley; felt somewhat sick all day after I

found it out. After we discovered it, the ship gave an extra roll and Clarence was in the receipt of the whole tureen in his lap—about a gallon. He said he did not mind eating them, but did not care to have them dumped all over him.
—Bement

Up at six to watch sea; so rough, could not sleep; thrown about in berth too much; had to jam my knees against the ceiling in order to stay in at all. Struck ice this morning and, of course, the sea went down. Great relief. Could not eat, read, sleep or anything else with any comfort *it* was so rough. *Had to hang on to berth to keep in.* Ice is East Greenland drift. It comes around Cape Farewell. No one on board ever heard of so much ice in this drift. It is very heavy and there are *many* seals on it. Church shot one. They are of harp and hooded varieties.

Spoke to Bridgman about the maggots, and he replied that that was nothing, he had them in the beef for several days. He was carving and so he could see. I had supposed the beef was larded. Held an indignation meeting with the captain, Cook and all but Bridgman. The captain appointed me chief steward *today*. About maggots, and beef and cabbage. Have had cabbage every meal. The steward is trying to run the ship, and I have to run the steward.

Crossed my farthest north (Alaska) today.[75] It is very light at 11:30 P.M. as we turn in. No sunset for several days on account of fog.
—Wyckoff

---

75.   Wyckoff's previous record had been Alaska.

THURSDAY, JULY 25TH, 1901

Up at 7:35 A.M. Found worms in the oatmeal. We are having a nice assortment of animals in our food. All of us paw over the grub, expect to find almost anything. These little things go to help ones appetites. Nit-hives [*sic*] troubled me all night. Both Wyckoff and I were in and out of our bunks all night long. Raining and foggy this morning. Nothing doing. Lots of bergs and pan ice. Bumped ice all night. It is getting monotonous. Can not get an observation; have not had one for 4 days. Our position is a matter of guess; dead reckoning by log, and that has been in part of the time on account of the ice. Sighted Greenland at 1 P.M. Everybody's spirits go up. Snow-capped mountains and the ice cap in back. The mountains were very high and peaked, and are above the clouds making the tops look as if they were floating in the air; a grand sight. Frederickshaab was our first sight of Greenland.
—Bement

In fairly clear water, icebergs about; took picture of an arch berg. Last night saw big berg turn over. Was not so much as I have heard tell. Went into [the] steward's stuff yesterday and found a lot of old stuff. He is saving new to sell when he gets back. Using barley which is very much off. *Bah!* So worm eaten that there are no kernels left; nothing but powder held together with the web of the worm. The rice is full of weevils.

Asked steward for his papers and found the best ship he ever sailed on was a cattle ship. He was educated in the slums of London. Is a cockney and his accent has been quite funny until now. He has no idea of cleanliness, and as the steward has entire charge of the stores and the cook has to serve what is given him. We have been getting the worst of everything. Our cook, by the way, is a nineteen-year-old boy, formerly a tailor's apprentice. As far as I can make out he has hardly ever seen a kitchen range before in his life, but he wanted to run away to sea, so we employed him as cook. Am making some changes, and the captain says he will back me up.

Have decided to make cook and steward change places. Damn the steward. New cook seems a trifle bull-headed. Insists on having plum duff *tomorrow* when I told him to serve it Sunday. Have a bum job. At 1:00 P.M. today we sighted Greenland. Many mountains and much snow on them. Clouds around peaks. It looks cold and bleak. [It is] now 11:10 P.M. [and] can see to read on deck. Sun set [at] 10:00 P.M. Have had no sight of sun for several days so could not take a reckoning. We are at least thirty miles out on our dead reckoning.
—Wyckoff

FRIDAY, JULY 26TH, 1901

Up at 7:45 A.M. Foggy and raining and generally nasty. Saw our first whale. Large one. The Doctor [Cook] is making preparations for the initiation of us [*sic*] who have never crossed the Arctic Circle. Church did the first washing so far. His clothes [are] hung up on the bow. No ice in sight; remarkable. Sunset last night at 10 P.M. and sunrise again at 11 P.M. Down just one hour. The grandeur of the sunset and sunrise beyond description; colors I never saw before so I give up description. Everybody downhearted this morning on account

Arch berg (W273)

"The first land we sighted was the west Greenland coast, somewhere south of Godhavn, and as soon as the captain got his bearings, he announced with great pride that he was only thirty miles out in his reckoning on crossing the bay. I understood later why he showed such pride at this time, as this was the nearest hit he made on the whole trip." (Wyckoff Notes)

The tailor's apprentice as cook (W19/B63)

"He started to desert and was only captured after he had gotten his trunk into a small boat and had started for the shore." (Wyckoff Notes)

Livestock on *Erik* (W152)

"The steward, who had entire charge of our provisions, was a cockney, born and bred in the slums of London. I had occasion afterwards to investigate his papers and found that the best job he had had before coming with us was as steward on board a cattle ship." (Wyckoff Notes)

of passing a mail steamer on its way to Copenhagen. Now we cannot tell when our letters will reach home, possibly not till next year; missed [the steamer] by one day. This steamer is the first sign of life we have seen since leaving the Gulf of St. Lawrence, a shipless ocean in fact. At 2 P.M. we crossed the Circle. The initiation immediately commenced. Dr. Cook in command.

Order #1—Wyckoff, Church and the Captain [Blakeney] lead the three sheep around the ship. It being a very rough day, it is a question [of], which lead, the sheep or the fellows. They were fit subjects of a bathtub by the time the job was completed. Great sport for the rest of us however.

Order #2—Stone was made to go below and dude up with a boiled shirt and collar. The balance of us retired to the engine room and smutted our hands up in elegant shape; and when poor Stone came on deck, we criticized the way he put his duds on and proceeded to adjust them correctly with our smutty and oily hands. By the time we were through with him he looked more like an end man than any thing else.

Order #3—Berri was made to strip the cabin boy and give him a bath—the first one we all decided he ever had. It was a hard job for

Trouble[76] but he succeeded with the captain's help and we discovered that the boy was originally white.

Order #4—Your Uncle Henry[77] was made to go on the bridge and deliver a speech to the entire ship's company. I had not much more [than] opened my mouth when it was immediately closed with a stale banana. Well, I never thought that there was as much stale fruit on board. All hands assisted.

I vow I never will throw any over ripe fruit at an actor again no matter how bad he may be. My speech was a complete failure. Now we are full-fledged Arctic men eligible for membership in the Arctic Club.

We saw a large porpoise run within 20 feet of the ship. After supper we saw an interesting sight. [It was] a fight between a very large whale and swordfish and thrasher (species of whale). The swordfish swims under the whale and by continual prodding, drives him to the surface. Then the thrasher rushes and leaps out of the water, same as a porpoise, and whacks him down again so the swordfish has an opportunity of giving him a good thrash. This they keep up until the whale is killed. Then they suck the blood from the whale. At times the swordfish misses the whale and he comes out of the water with great force. Being all large fish they lash the ocean into foam.

76. Bement's nickname for Herbert Berri.

77. Bement's nickname for himself.

Crossing the Arctic Circle (W54)

l. to r. Wyckoff, Church, Bement, Stone, and Berri dress up for their initiation ceremony.

In the evening we had a punch bowl in celebration of crossing the Circle. We all drank to the health of our families and friends, as well as [to the] success to Peary and our expedition. Snowed at 10 P.M. Rained and foggy nearly all day. The coast hardly in sight. *Temperature* [is] 35°F, at 10:30 P.M., and broad daylight.

—Bement

Down in the hold showing new steward the stores and explaining his duties. Did not know anything about any of it myself; it is a nice job. Have discovered that this boat, which at one time belonged to the Hudson Bay Company, was wrecked and left on the rocks for three years while they were adjusting the insurance. This is her first trip since she was repaired. We purchased what provisions were on her, and as near as I can make out, some of the stuff was with her through the wreck. It certainly looks the part.

Crossed Arctic Circle. Had initiation. Captain [Blakeney], Church, and myself had to lead our three live sheep around in the rain and on slippery decks. Louie had to make speech from bridge—pelted with bum, very bum, bananas. It was a bum speech. Berri had to wash the cabin boy with soap and water. It was a good job and was needed. Stone dressed in boiled shirt and collar, and all hands turned in and gave him a reception with sooted hands.

11:35 P.M. Writing in cabin without a light. Had a weak punch because we crossed [the Arctic] circle. Saw whales, swordfish, porpoise, and thrasher. The thrasher and swordfish had combined to kill the whale. The thrasher is a big sort of fish with a very big tail, and every time the whale came above water to breathe, the thrasher would soak him with his tail; as he dove to escape the thrasher, the swordfish would strike him from underneath forcing him back to Mr. Thrasher again. The sailors say such a fight is liable to last for days and probably ends in the death of the whale.

It has been very rough. Sea following nine and one half knots.

—Wyckoff

SATURDAY, JULY 27TH, 1901

Foggy, rain and snow, we crawled up the coast slowly opposite Disco Island at 11:00 A.M. Extremely heavy sea blowing a gale and snowing hard which cut the face like small stones. Unable to find Disco Fjord; came about and ran back to a fjord we had passed to get out of the storm. What a relief to get into smooth water. All our gear down on the floor in the cabin; an awful mess. Dropped anchor at 12 P.M. Blew the whistle at intervals and kept a sharp lookout for Huskies.[78] In about two hours we made out five specks on the water. In a short time they took the shape of men in their kayaks and soon they were alongside. The water was

---

78. "Husky" was a word used interchangeably with "Eskimo" to describe the native people. They called themselves "Inuit," however, even as early as 1901 (see Editorial Note, p. xiii).

Five men board the *Erik* (W230/B10)

*"I shall not attempt to give you my ideas of these people on my
first visit ashore. Besides, my ideas would possibly be affected by
the remembrance of the blisters I raised on that twenty-mile row."*
(Wyckoff Notes)

rough and went completely over them. [It was] a mystery how they kept afloat. We dropped two ropes with noose in end and they slipped them over bow and stern of their kayaks, and we started the steam wench a going and hauled them aboard. [It] took us about an hour to get them all on deck.

This was our first introduction to Huskies. None of them would take a prize in a beauty show, and as for odor, I did not suppose a human being could live and stink so, but facts prove themselves and we had the facts. Clarence said he could smell them the length of the ship and he to the windward and I guess he is correct. However, the doctor [Cook] tells us that they do not smell half as bad as the northern Eskimos. "God help us." The doctor oiled up his Husky and after an hour's work, managed to find out that their settlement was about 6 miles up the fjord and that Godhavn, our destination, was a few miles north. One of them offered to act as pilot for us in the morning. It is strange what a nose for scent the Husky has. He found the galley at once and you could not drive them [*sic*] away. The cook had orders to fill them up, which he did. Their capacity for grub of all kinds except salt food is enormous. These men were dressed in sealskin trousers reaching just below the knees, and seal jackets like a sweater with a hood on it which covers the head leaving part of the face exposed, sealskin boots, and seal mittens. All had sore eyes and repulsive-looking long black hair. They were [a] copper color.

Their boats, or kayaks, were 16 feet long, 2 feet amidship, made of sealskin. They sit in the bottom of the boat, and the deck, in a light sea, is always underwater. They use an arrangement about 18 inches high made of sealskin [that is] circular [and] which fits over the opening in the boat, and reaches up under the arms. Then they have a lightweight skin like an oilskin they draw over the head and shoulders down over the heavier one, which makes a watertight arrangement, making it impossible for any water to get into the boat so no matter how heavy a sea they have, it is impossible to sink them. Strapped on the boat is their harpoon, lance, snow knife, skinning knife, and harpoon line holder. About seven P.M. we decided to row up to their settlement. Bridgman, Cook, Wyckoff, Church, Berri, myself, two sailors and two Huskies, started in the whaleboat. It was raining hard so [we] got into our oilskins and had our first experience with a 17 lb. 16 ft. oar in a whaleboat. We earned our passage. [We] arrived in about two hours and if the Huskies had not been along, would never have found the place as the huts are made of earth and moss, same as the ground. They soon saw us and the whole settlement was out to meet us all dressed in their brightest and best skins. Had hard work landing on account of the rocks and surf. Many willing hands assisted and we got all of our trading stuff ashore.

The settlement [was] comprised of 63 people and about 15 igloos (huts): some round, others square. Every Husky insisted upon your getting down on your hands and knees and crawling from 6 to 10 feet through the entrance into the igloo. Their being very short, they could slide in without much trouble but take us 6 footers [and] it was difficult. Our gear was carried up into one hut; [it was] the largest one, about 10 feet square, and the whole population insisted upon going in. The smell was enough to drive one to the high timbers before they came in,

Lievely Harbor, Disko (W329)

*"The name of this scattered settlement of huts, Godhaven [sic], comes
clearly enough, from its offering fortunate refuge from storms; that the place
is also known as Lively [sic] is not in the least to be wondered at, if one
has watched a midnight dance of the little population and their visitors."*
(Cook, My Attainment of the Pole, 37)

Ootoonioksuah (B299) FAC

Inuk from Cape York.

Inuit dwelling made of stone and turf (B16)

Inuit women tanning skins by chewing (B283)

and after they were there a few minutes, it was something awful and we moved out. We traded for trinkets, 5 ship biscuits, being the standard or legal tender. Some of the women were fine looking, even pretty, and all had teeth that we envied; even the old. [Their teeth were] even, white, and perfect. I found out the smell was from the skins they wore more than from a bodily filth. This [smell of the skins] is from the way they are tanned, being chewed by the women. However, they never take a bath. They had some magnificent dogs, and they [the dogs] seem to live on fighting. Found an old couple who could speak a little English and they said that they had been to New York City and I asked them to describe it. They said mountains, high igloos, and large dogs drawing sleds, meaning high buildings and horses and wagons. Dr. Cook informed me afterward that he doubted it very much, but that they had heard the whalers talk about it years ago and they did that to get grub. We left this interesting place at 11:30 P.M. and reached the ship about 1:30 A.M. after a hard pull. It was as light as day. We have said goodbye to nights now till next September.

—Bement

Still very rough. Sighted Disko Island on which is situated Godhaven. Ran by Godhaven harbor and decided to anchor in Disko Bay until the storm abated. We were making about twelve knots before the wind with all sails set. It was necessary to take in sails before we could turn into the Bay, and it required all six sailors, the two mates, and our former cabin boy up aloft. The captain asked me to take [the] wheel and I had to have three[79] assistants to keep the ship on her course. It was snowing a sleety nasty kind of snow, and with the gale and all it was a very nasty job standing at the wheel. The Erik is so light in ballast, her head is way out of water, and it is a pretty difficult thing to steer her by compass. She yawed about and veered over five points, fully 60° to 70°. It was only after we had gotten into the bay that we discovered we had run by Godhaven, as all on board thought we were making [it] into that harbor. *Ran into Disko Fyjord. Too rough to find Godhaven with its small harbor.* Anchored until morning.

Disko Fiord is a large bay and a splendid harbor in such a combined storm and fog, as we have just passed through.

Five Huskies came in kayaks. Hoisted them on board, boat and all, as they could not get out of kayaks until they were on a solid foundation. They were practically tied into their boat with a band of sealskin, which completely covered the only opening in the boat and came up under their armpits. This construction making an airtight craft. If a Husky tips over he has no way of saving himself from drowning unless others come to his assistance as there is no way that he can get out of his boat while in the water. The five stated that there was a village of sixty-three people at the other end of the bay, so Louis, Doctor [Cook], *Burt,*[80] two engineers, Bridgman, and myself got into the gig whaleboat,

79. The original diary said two assistants. When Wyckoff dictated the expanded diary, he changed the number to three.

80. Burt was Wyckoff's nickname for Herbert Berri.

and with the help of two or three Huskies rowed over to the village. This was the first time we had the six-oared whaleboat out, and it is a gentle little craft. On our return, to settle an argument I had with the first mate, we weighted one of the oars and it tipped the scales at a little over seventeen pounds. I rowed oar practically all of the way to the village *(against a head wind),* while the others changed about. Several blisters and bum wrist. The distance proved to be only about ten miles. It was certainly exasperating to see the Huskies trying to go slow enough in their kayaks to keep pace with us. They apparently made no exertion at all, while we were laboring all of the time.

When we arrived at the village there was a big *gang* to meet us all dressed up in their Sunday furs and clothes of all colors: red, yellow, green seem to predominate. Twenty of the Huskies grabbed hold of the big whaleboat and drew her way up on [the] beach.

The dwellings of the Huskies were made of mud with some wood in evidence. A long tunnel served as entrance and it is so small that you have to crawl in. Berri [got] stuck in one of the tunnels and had to be pulled out. You cannot stand up inside of the houses. The women were quite pretty and the whole show was very picturesque, though on close acquaintance, quite dirty. Could take no pictures on account of fog. All the Eskimos in this Danish section of Greenland are half-breeds: *Danes.* We returned to the ship by 1 A.M., after purchasing

fish, ducks, and numbers of trinkets. There is no darkness tonight although owing to the fog, and later the snowstorm, we have not seen the sun. *Large harbor here. Fine anchorage. Very hard snowstorm today.*
—Wyckoff

SUNDAY, JULY 28TH, 1901
We arrived at Godhaven at 11 A.M. After laying outside and whistling some time for a pilot. All the settlements in this country are situated back from the coast some miles up a fjord, thus Godhave[n]. The channel is very narrow and lined with rocks. After letting go the anchor, the ship was immediately swarming with Huskies and they made for the galley the first thing. The cook had some grease he turned out into cans to cool and they commenced to eat that stuff by the hand full and would have finished it if they had not been driven away. Each Husky carried some sort of bundle, which they [*sic*] soon exposed for sale. All kinds of ivory work, small kayaks, beadwork, etc. We could not understand them, but soon got onto their sign language and then the fun began. We had no Danish money so [we] traded ship biscuits, clothes, tobacco, etc. for this stuff.

The Governor[81] [Nielsen] came aboard and dined with us, and gave us permission to go ashore, as soon as he found out we had no diseases. We returned his call. At 3 P.M., before we left the ship, we cleared it of all the Huskies. The governor set

81. The governor of Godhavn from 1901–1904 was Christian August Nielsen (correspondence with Leif Vanggaard of Arktisk Institut [the Danish Arctic Institute], Copenhagen, Denmark).

Arriving at Godhavn (W235)

"Governor came on board just in time for dinner. Could talk a little English and little German. Very interesting dinner: English, Dutch, Danish, Eskimo and French mixed in." (Wyckoff Diary)

Stone house, Godhavn (W242)

"Oh, mother, how funny it is to look over there and see only a few frame houses one and a half stories high, a tiny frame church with a school-bell on top, and then only mounds of turf with a window stuck in the end of each and a chimney on one side,-and to think this is a capital city!" [Marie Peary, Children of the Arctic *(New York: Frederick A. Stokes Company, 1903), 24–25]*

Godhavn, Disko Island (W229)

up the wine, brandy, and cigars; also a small lunch. We drank to everybody's health and all were extremely polite. Mailed our letters and changed $75 in English gold to Danish money.

1 krone[82] bill equal to	.28 our money
50 ore bill equal to	.14 our money
25 ore bill equal to	.07 our money

Then in copper 5 Ores, 2 Ores, 1 ore, 1/2 ore

As soon as we got out, we were offered all kinds of stuff for our money, and if anybody thinks that these half civilized people are not sharp in a trade, they are mistaken. They beat a down east Yankee.

Seal jackets:	5 kroner
Seal pants:	5 kroner
Kayaks:	2 or 3 kroner
Harpoons:	3 to 5 kroner
Spears:	3 kroner
Bead necklaces:	4 to 5 kroner
Small bone/ivory trinkets:	a handful of candy

These are the prices established by us and we forced the market and soon had everything bought up. Wyckoff bought a large kayak for 2 English pounds ($10.00). The price of labor for 12 to 18 hours work is 1 krone or 28 cents. I was appointed

the one to carry the candy and they are very fond of it, both young and old, and the greatest beggars on earth. By giving each one two to three pieces, we got them to pose for us so [we] could take their pictures and it was great sport. All we could compare them with was the feeding of chickens. They divided up with each other showing an unselfish disposition. The babies are called "mick-ininny"[83] same as in the south. We noticed that the dogs were not nearly as fine as at the Disco Fjord settlement but just as ferocious. The women were all dressed in bright colors and lots of beadwork. Some of the young girls were good-looking but the old women were hideous, all wrinkled up. We were informed that the Eskimos were getting up a dance for our benefit so all hands are going ashore again. Back to the ship at 6 P.M. Had supper and ashore again at 8 P.M.; bought more stuff. Church got a fine pair of dog skin boots for 8 kroner; Cook a fur sleeping bag [for the] same price they got them from the Danish people. The dance took place in the carpenter shop. Music by a fiddler. The dance is on the order of our square dance, balancing and then swing. They keep time with a shuffling motion of the feet like a buck dancer[84] passing from one to the other. Any number can dance. They form a circle. Some of our sailors danced with them and it amused them to see them jig with their heavy boots. The Huskies wearing skin boots sounded like two pieces of sand paper being rubbed together.

---

82. An aluminum bronze coin and monetary unit of Denmark equal to 100 ore and approximately twelve cents in U.S. currency in 2001.

83. Inuit word for babies, it was defined in Bement's handwritten Inuit language dictionary.

84. Buck and wing was a tap dance derived in style from Black and Irish clog dances, marked especially by vigorous hopping, flinging of the legs and clicking of the heels.

Godhaven consists of five wooden buildings for the governor [Nielsen] and about 50 Eskimo huts. We visited their burial ground, which was enclosed with a picket fence, which was in good repair, [and] which seemed strange to us, on account of the scarcity of wood here. The temptation to the Huskies must be great. We leave this interesting place tomorrow. All would like to stay a few days and see more of this northern life. We are getting used to the Husky smell. All back to the ship by 11:30 P.M.
—Bement

Weighed anchor before I was up and started for Godhaven. When I went on deck we were outside of harbor. Had two pilots from the fjord and found a boat waiting with nine more. *All Huskies.* Could [not] have gone in without one. Fine entrance. High land and deep water. Landed after breakfast. All the time here had trouble with the new cook. I would order chicken soup and he would have bean soup, especially if we had baked beans with it. Natives here are very Danish. Some wear European clothes. Have much wood, but most of the houses have sod walls, while they use wood for the roofs, floors, and interior. They have a raised floor at one end of the house for sleeping. They use iron stoves and crockery. A Greenland issue of Danish money is used for trading.

Governor Nielsen and the Inspector live in fine wood houses. They have a store here where the natives can get many European articles. Girls and dogs not as fine looking as the Disko Fiord lot, but Bement and Stone did not seem to notice the difference.

Spent the day taking photos and buying native things. Most of the natives wear seal and dog trousers and shoes. Day poor for taking photos; got few good ones. Bought complete suit of fur clothing with all the extras dead and alive. Bought complete kayak outfit for two [English] pounds.

Suit costs:

Trousers	five kroner
Coat	eight kroner
Shoes	five kroner

One krone costs about twenty-eight cents.

The *Governor* came on board just in time for dinner. He could talk a little English and little German. Very interesting dinner: English, Dutch, Danish, Eskimo and French mixed in. No news of Peary or Windward. Later an Eskimo said that the Windward was lost and Mrs. Peary was at Upernavik.

On landing [we] went through Governor's house and were nicely treated. He served wine and brandy. English gold is the best medium. Exchanged one pound for 18 kroner and 18 ore. The Governor had a fine home-like house, but the rooms were lined with heavy paper.

Harpoons cost three kroner. At Disko Fiord five ship biscuits would buy any one thing. An Eskimo will apparently sell anything for a price. When I bought the kayak, the Eskimo would not go down in price but kept throwing in extras.

More trouble with the cook.
—Wyckoff

Governor Nielsen standing in front of his house (W237)

MONDAY, JULY 29TH, 1901

Up at 7:30 A.M. first day of sunshine since leaving Port aux Basques. Warm and fine. Everybody ashore except Church and myself. The Huskies filling the water tank. Anchor up at 9:00 A.M. and out we go through the Viagat. All the Huskies in Godhaven on shore waving goodbye. The Viagat is the inside passage between Disco Island and the mainland about 120 miles. Elegant day. Everybody on deck in shirtsleeves. Grand scenery; beautiful coloring. I thought I had seen icebergs but they were mini gobs, along side of these we saw today both in size and design. We counted 178 minimum bergs to say nothing of the hundreds of small ones. Did not count anything smaller than our house to as large as from the Ithaca Hotel to Treman's.[85] You could see every design from a duck to a castle. It is now 11 P.M. and I am writing in the cabin with a light. This is the first night of the midnight sun, at 71° latitude.
—Bement

After taking a few more pictures ashore, we sailed early this morning for Upernavik via the Vaigot. *Wonderful panorama of bergs.* The trip through the Vaigot was the most wonderful ice panorama imaginable. Dr. Cook stated that he had never seen its equal north or south. We had a remarkable [*sic*] fine day. Good sunlight until 10:30 P.M. *Could see the sunlight on clouds and high mountains all night.* It is very light all night long and I took a few photos at

midnight. *Took pictures at 12:20, the darkest we had it.* It is now 1:30 A.M. and growing very light.

I counted 187 large bergs all in sight at one time. The shores were lined with glaciers and altogether it is the most typical Arctic scenery we have yet come across. Some of the bergs have very peculiar shapes. Have seen one immense cave in a berg from 200 to 300 feet in height. Another took the form of an immense amphitheater. We have seen many arch bergs. In fact, they have been unusually common. Have passed many eider ducks and if we could have taken time to stop could have shot any quantity. I am told that this section through here is typical of all of Greenland. Everywhere along the coast you are in sight of snow. Most of the winter snow, however, melts along the coast and there is a margin of from 25 to 60 miles, which is practically barren of everything except rocks. Inside all that and always visible from the coast the ice cap begins. Once on an ice cap and there is nothing but snow and ice until you get to the coast again. In the interior the cap rises in places to a height of 1200 feet above sea level. There is practically no vegetation; a small bushy growth is frequently seen, called a willow.

At Godhaven we found a little grass, some moss, and a number of small flowers. I have seen it stated that there are forty-two varieties of flowers along this coast. The one most in evidence is the poppy.

Have had more trouble in my official capacity as chief steward. With everything run in four-hour

85. Treman Brothers Hardware, a four-story structure, was located at 101–107 East State Street in Ithaca, New York. Approximately two city blocks away stood the Ithaca Hotel.

Monarch of the north (W358)

Iceberg along the coast (W337)

Stopping at Upernavik (W175/B56) FAC

l. to r. Church, Stone, Berri, and Bement.

Ice spire (C18)

Glorious light (W308/B236)

"You could see every design from a duck to a castle." (Bement Diary)

Wyckoff (left) and Church sunbathing (B104/W90)

watches, it is absolutely necessary to have meals on time. At twelve today, the dinner hour, I went up to the galley and found our new cook baking bread. Dinner was an hour late. I consulted with the officers and found out that Second Mate Will Bartlett once served as steward on a sailing vessel. He consented to act as our steward. So I arranged with the captain to "break" and "log" the cockney cook, and put him before the mast. The tailor's apprentice has gone back as cook, and we have taken a sailor *(Tom)* from before the mast and made him second mate. I trust there will be no more change. I have forgotten to mention that we had to fire our cabin boy, not from the ship, but into the stoke hold. He was alive with vermin and not fit for polite society.

Sun set in the magnetic north, in true northwest at 10:30. Latitude 70°N.
—Wyckoff

TUESDAY, JULY 30TH, 1901
Up at 7:40, grand day, elegant bergs, arch ones. About 500 pictures were taken yesterday. Eider duck[86] for dinner yesterday. Ptarmigan duck[87] today. Living high. Midnight sun last night. Mountains look as if they were capped with sheet. Got a bath; bedding all out on deck. Cleaned up room; hung everything up [that was] on the floor. As usual five

letters today. Sailor did washing. Saw Yosemite Falls and Taughannock.[88] Mr. Bridgman fell through the hatch. Berri [given] permission to take a bath tomorrow.

Through Viagat at 4 A.M. Open sea again. Wyckoff wrote four letters; hardest job of his life. Been talking about it for 14 days.[89] Coast bold rocky red; 1000 to 3000 feet high. Grand. Everybody to bed early to be up at 6 A.M. to take in Upernivik. Have a fine crop of whiskers. Berri to sleep on deck tonight. Duck by the thousand. Longitude 55° 20', Latitude 73°.
—Bement

It is a fine day. Temperature 40°F. Everyone is around on deck in shirtsleeves. The coldest we have at all is 34°F. While down in the hold working with the new steward, Mr. Bridgman fell down the hatch but was not much hurt. My new duties seem to keep me busy all of the time and I have to plan all meals. *General sun today. Ice. Mountains covered with snow. Busy every minute with one thing and another.*
—Wyckoff

WEDNESDAY, JULY 31ST, 1901
Up at 7:30 A.M.; dropped anchor at 4 A.M. at Upernivik. Governor [Kraul] and northern Inspector[90] [Jensen] call on us at breakfast time.

---

86. Any of several large sea ducks of the genus *Somateria*, the females of which yield eiderdown. They also are one of the most common food birds of Inuit.
87. Any of several grouses of the genus *Lagopus*, of mountainous and cold northern regions having feathered feet. They are among the most abundant and most widely used food birds of Inuit.

88. Taughannock is the Ithaca, New York, version of Yosemite Falls. Probably a joke about the amount of water pouring down the hatch.
89. Probably a joke about how difficult it was for Wyckoff to write.
90. Referring to J. Daugaard Jensen, the governor and inspector from 1900–1912 [correspondence with Leif Vanggaard of the Arktisk Institut (Danish Arctic Institute), Copenhagen, Denmark].

Arriving at Upernavik (B57)

l. to r. Church, Bement, and Stone

Upernavik (W228/B25) FAC

" . . . a great rock cliff, loomed upon the horizon. Beyond it, gradually appeared a long chain of those islands among which lies Upernavik, where the last traces of civilized or semi-civilized life are found." (Cook, My Attainment of the Pole, *38)*

Inuit at Upernavik (W209)

Women wear sealskin trousers, decorated with a front strip of skin embroidery. The woman with the white boots wears the traditional West Greenlandic deep beaded collar and the style of knotting her hair in a topknot with a headband color that indicates her marital status. She wears the collar, cuffs and stocking tops made of imported European black ox fur.

Mother and five children at Upernavik (B23)

"Nearly all the natives of Danish Greenland wear clothing made of woven material, for which they trade their furs and blubber with the Danish people who govern them and teach them." (Marie Peary, Children of the Arctic, *1903, 30.)*

Two women and two children (W212)

"The Eskimos are a friendly lot and one soon picks up enough of their language to make your wants known . . ." (Bement Notes)

Ashore at 9 A.M. Mailed bunch of letters.

Bought jacket—5 kroner. Saw dogs fed (twice a week). Glass of wine with the Governor [Kraul]. Introduced to his wife. Took [a] lot of pictures. No souvenirs here at all. Huskies dirtier and smell stronger than those at Godhaven.

Getting out the ammunition this morning. Lifted anchor at 10:30 and left the last signs of civilization behind. Heard at U[pernavik] that the Windward was seen in March fast in the ice trying to get north. Bad news. Bridgman and Cook think it must have been the Fram.[91] We are rushing north now; expect to find things in bad shape so that means our hunting cut short. This Expedition is the first of the 20th Century. Inspector's name [is] Jonneson [Jensen]; Governor [is] Knauft.[92] Church dressed up in his Husky suit and went aloft to look out for bears. Everybody all tired out. We ran into the ice again at 1 P.M. and bumped it until 7:30 P.M. Then got on inside of pack. Now among the large bergs which is better.
—Bement

Arrived Upernavik before I was up. Not much of interest here. Very similar to Godhaven. The natives *stink more and* are dirtier and the odor is more pronounced than before. There is a population of from 160 to 200, mostly living in mud huts. There is not as much wood as in evidence at Godhaven. Inspector Jensen seems a fine fellow, is young, and

speaks good English. The natives will do anything for candy. *Took a good many photos.*
—Wyckoff

THURSDAY, AUGUST 1ST, 1901

Foggy, pleasant, frosty warm, and cold. Up at 7:30 A.M. Appointed two-hour lookout for bears. Each taking turn. Sighted three bears at 2 P.M.; old one and two cubs. Everybody overboard on the ice and after them; [went] in 500 yards and they saw us and started off. A general firing commenced until out of range. Then everybody started on a run after them. Sun shining brightly. Could see for miles and as quick as I can write this, a fog came down on us and we could not see bears, ship or anybody. Commenced to holler to each other after a spell. Got all together but could not see the ship. We were a mile and a half away on an ice pan full of seal holes and could not see 10 feet away. They [the *Erik*] blew the whistle, and got under way, and came around the pan nearer to us and we fired our guns. Came together at last; got aboard and the fog lifted. We could see the bears off about two miles away but gave up the chase and started north again through the ice. Fog one minute and sun the next, as quick as they can shift scenery. We bunted ice and at last got caught in between two pans and only had about 40 feet to go for open water. It took us 5 hours to make it. We tried to cut it with axes, but it was too thick so [the ship] kept bucking

---

91. Norwegian ship led by polar explorer and scientist, Fridtjof Nansen, who, from 1893–96, led an expedition across the Greenland inland ice that received international attention.

92. Text appears as Knauft. However, Hans Peter Kraul was the governor of Upernavik from 1896–1910 [correspondence with Leif Vanggaard of the Arktisk Institut (Danish Arctic Institute), Copenhagen, Denmark].

Fred Church (W63)

Men loosening the ice around *Erik* (W103/B177)

"The ice was extra heavy and we were held up for several days,
putting us in training for the heavier ice we were to meet later on."
(Bement Notes)

Frederick Cook in the crow's nest (W122)

*He selects a course through the drifting ice and then shouts his orders to
the officers on the ship's bridge.*

up and bunting it, gaining about a foot a whack, when the wind shifted and closed up the channel entirely and we had to get another pan and cut the ice away from the sides of the ship to relieve the pressure. All of a sudden Berri sighted the three bears again coming toward us. All rushed for their guns and waited but Mr. Bears sighted us and off they went. They were fully a mile away when they saw us. We did not go after them as they could out foot us. My watch [is] from 2 to 4. Nothing doing; too foggy to see. I am on again from 12:00 A.M. till 2 A.M. up in the crow's-nest. Most accommodating ship you ever saw. Stops to let us go bear hunting, goes out of her course to let us take pictures.

We are now, and have been all day, in Melville Bay. May be out tomorrow and may be icebound for one or two weeks. This is the hardest and most dangerous part of the trip. After we reach cape [Cape York] we have 200 miles more to go but it will be all open sea. The hives trouble me so that I have been on deck for the past 3 nights for a half hour to 1 hour in my pajamas, bathrobe, and slip-pers, from 12 to 1 o'clock. So it demonstrates that the weather is not very cold, and [the] ship going full speed.
—Bement

This morning we ran into the Melville Bay pack ice. For quite a while we thought we were stuck, but the seam we were wedged into widened and let us through. The only way we can make headway here is by conning the ship. One man stays in the crow's-nest and picks out a course through the drifting ice and shouts his orders to the officers on the bridge, who in turn directs the helmsman. It is a case of hammer and shove to get through some of the narrow openings.

At one o'clock three polar bears were sighted on the ice; she bear and two cubs. They were on an immense floe, which we had been skirting, and the ship was rammed into the ice, ladders let down, and ten or fifteen people, started after them. At least ten people had guns, and they all began to bang away at long range. *All missed.* Of course, the bears ran away and we lost them. Church, Bement, and myself started inland over the ice after them, but had not gone far before a fog settled down and we were obliged to find our way back to the ship. Later in the day, about three o'clock, we saw three more bears, but had no chance for a shot on account of the fog. At eleven P.M. another bear was sighted, the biggest we had seen yet. It was no use to go for him however because of the dense fog.

We are now taking regular two-hour watches on the crow's nest on the watch for bear. I had from 12:00 to 2:00 pm. and 10:00 to 12:00 pm. *Go on 8 to 10 and 6 to 4 tomorrow.* I had a shot at four of the bears but at such a long range it was absolutely hopeless. *Damn the fog. All very long range.*
—Wyckoff

FRIDAY, AUGUST 2ND, 1901
My watch [is] from 12 to 2 A.M. At 11:50 A.M., Wyckoff called down bear. Asleep, all dressed up. Grabbed gun on deck, first one. Heavy fog; saw bear on pan, just made out his outline in the fog. We all shot twice. Wyckoff and Church went over-board after him. We started the ship for other side. He got away in the fog. They did not dare follow him on account of soft ice. Seven bears we have

Wyckoff and Church on bear watch (B248)

"Our polar bear hunting was a failure. Saw seven but at the time did not have dogs to hold them at bay. They swam from ice pan to ice pan and got away from our guns." (Bement Notes)

Skinning a seal (B71)

*Bement (left) and Church (bending over) at work while Wardwell, and
a sailor (right) look on. The skinning took all day.*

seen and no bear aboard yet. My watch, going at 1/2 speed. Large pan of ice appeared on port bow. In getting away from it, we nearly crashed into an immense iceberg. With full force astern, and hard to port, we just grazed it. Narrow escape. First real scare we have had. Midnight sun appeared through fog and clouds. Getting brighter every minute; soft mellow light of yellow cast. As it got brighter, the sky turned to a light blue, grand in colors; brighter until fog and clouds disappeared and it came forth as bright as any summer day. Had to put on blue goggles to see on account of the sun shining on the ice. Sun in the east and a bright moon in the west; such a grand midnight sun.

I decided to continue to stand watch and at 2:10 the first mate [Moses Bartlett] told me that there was a seal on a little berg on port bow. I ran to the bow, and saw him, and shot. Struck him just over front flippers. He rolled over to get into the water and I shot again sending a ball through the brain. He continued to flop, shot twice more and hit him each time in the body. I first shot 100 yards, second 150, 3rd and 4th about 200 [yards]. [We] lowered the boat [and] two sailors got him aboard. Weighed about 250 lbs. First game aboard except ducks. Congratulations from all. Turned in at 3:15 A.M.

Up at 7:40 A.M. After breakfast Church and I skinned the seal. Took us until dinnertime to get the skin off. After dinner we got the blubber off the skin. It ranged from 1 to 2 inches thick. Terrific job. Did not finish until 4:30 P.M. Salted down the skin. Washed up. Would not skin another for all of the seals in Melville Bay. We have been bumping ice nearly all day. Got out at 4 P.M. In open water opposite Sabine Islands. At 6 P.M. from our present position can see 60 miles distance, and farther, if any land about. No fog today; remarkable.
—Bement

Latitude 75° 30'. Longitude 61° 10'. Temperature below freezing. 1:15 A.M. Louie is on watch. Fog is very thick although the sun occasionally breaks through and we would see a midnight sun were it not for the fog. *Just took pictures of sun.* Narrowly escaped running into an iceberg, the highest one we have yet seen. During my watch in the crow's nest, the engineer asked me to get him some coffee. *I have entire charge of stores.* I went up to the galley and found it full of smoke. The cook had left the beans on the hot stove and they were burned to a crisp and the kettle broken *and cracked.* I had to get the cook up and boil more beans for breakfast. *Damn being chief steward!* 3:00 A.M. it is so light all the time that no one knows when to go to bed. Louis just killed a seal. Stopped long enough to bring him on board. We have been in and out of the ice all day long and it is simply a case of breaking our way through—full speed ahead—full speed astern and try again.

At 12:00 *midnight* we arrived off Cape York where there are two towns of the northern tribe of Eskimo. These are the most southern of the full blood Eskimos. Melville Bay being the dividing line between them and the Danish Eskimo. We blew the whistle several times and both towns turned out with dog sledges and kayaks. Luckily it was light enough to take many pictures. These people are entirely different from the South Greenland bunch. They are savage looking and filthy dirty. Wear bearskin trousers and sealskin upper garments.

Midnight sun (2:00 AM) at Cape York (B282)

Inuit waiting for Erik *to anchor to the ice.*

A number came on board and I took to the rigging. I thought we had found odors among the southern Huskies but these easily carried off the palm. It was rather difficult to realize it, but these people have absolutely nothing to live with and on except the animals they kill, the stones they make their huts of, and the ice and snow, with a few grasses and mosses that one finds on the coast. *As far as I could see, there was absolutely no vegetation at all at this point.* There are no conveniences here and one should not blame them perhaps for their filthy conditions, nevertheless mine for the rigging. *Took many pictures.*

We left at 2:15 A.M. after arranging to keep one man, three dogs, two women, and a kid. *Bah! All four went to bed in a sailor's single bunk; all naked.* These people live in a town alongside of a glacier, and it must be worse than a dog's life they lead. —Wyckoff

SATURDAY, AUGUST 3RD, 1901

Stayed up last night until 3:30 A.M. Rammed the ice to an anchorage. Sighted Cape York 60 miles away. Captain [Blakeney] claims 75 [miles]. Whistled for some time; shortly about 75 Huskies lined the shore, [we] dropped a ladder, and over they came. They all knew Dr. Cook and Mr. Bridgman and they were very excited. The cat and sheep attracted their attention. Loaded them up with ship biscuits, and cleared the ship of them. Almost every woman had a baby strapped on her back and all the mickininnies had on was a seal jacket; the hood supplied the balance. They would take them out to nurse and they were bare from the waist down, and this they do all winter. The people's clothing

Cape York Inuit on deck (B288)
Wife of Kaiotah (right), child, and young girl of sixteen.
(Bement Log)

Inuit tupik [tent] (B306) FAC

Showing skins drying and sealskin float used in hunting.

Billy Bah, girl of 16 (W386/B319)

Her Inuit name was Eklaylshoo [Ikklayoshoo] but Marie Peary could not pronounce her name so she gave her the name "Billy Bah." Eklaylshoo [Ikklayoshoo] was the wife of Ahngoodloo. Also known as "Miss Bill," she was one of the Inuit taken to the United States in 1894 by Mrs. Peary and returned the following year. (Bement Log)

consists of a seal jacket and bearskin pants, which while standing does not quite meet, showing their bellies and backs. They are the nastiest and strongest smelling things I've ever come in contact with and full of lice of all kinds. One woman went over the side of the ship [and] with a baby one week old on her back, [she climbed] down a rope. Habits of confinement. We got a Husky, his wife and baby, 3 dogs, [a] kayak and sled, also a young girl, 17 years old, to go to Etah with us. Their young to bed in forecastle.

When a woman has had a miscarriage, she has to wear a hood and mittens until the next sun or moon. When in mourning, [she] can [not] put meat in a pot to cook or take out, unless she has a son and [he] takes hold of her wrist while so doing. When laboring with childbirth, she has to go into a separate igloo and have it all alone, except at birth [when] an old woman attends her. She gets up and is about in a day or two. A Husky has the right to exchange [his] wife or trade her for anything he wishes. When a woman dies and leaves a child under three years, the husband has option of killing the child if he wishes. When a boy, they learn one [or] two customs to follow through life. One [custom] is not to eat your Arctic hare before it has turned white.[93]

At 2 P.M. today we started. Wyckoff, Church, Stone, Berri, and myself, with Huskies to a big rock, (Dalrymple),[94] [for] duck hunting. [We went] ashore at 3 P.M. and [the] fun commenced. Got 62 eider ducks in less than 2 hours. Just bang, bang, all the time. Each used about 50 cartridges apiece, shot about every 5th bird (discussion of rock and birds). Back to the ship at 5 P.M. Shoulder sore and all tired out. Going to bed early, and take off my clothes—first time in four nights. Etah tomorrow; the end of the journey; there for hunting.
—Bement

[At] 8:00 A.M. the Doctor [Cook] came down with the cry of bear, but was lying. He got up after three hours sleep and I had been up twenty hours at a stretch before. *Chess: Stone 21 to 10.*

Dr. Cook has been able to get a little information from these Eskimos, but it is three months old as they can only travel on the ice along the shore when everything is frozen up [*sic*]. They say that Peary is not at Etah but is north of there with the Windward; we can not tell just where. Mr. Bridgman got a letter which he had sent to Mr. Peary in March via Dundee whalers.

10:40. We passed Petowik Glacier today which authority has said is fifteen miles long. It was only three miles long by our log. Stopped at Dalrymple Island for fresh meat. Shot sixty-two eider ducks and guillemots. The birds flew about as if crazy and we stood in the open without any attempt at concealment, and fired at them as they circled the island.

---

93. This paragraph was written on an end page of Bement's diary, however, he intended that it be inserted here.

94. Dalrymple Rock, now a bird sanctuary, was in 1901 a favorite spot for hunting and egg collecting because of the large eider colony there.

Robert Peary checking a woman for head lice (W101)

The *Erik* at Dalrymple Rock (B239) FAC
Known as the rookery of eider ducks, it is today a bird sanctuary.

Dr. Cook says Eskimos will pull out a louse and eat him. If he is small, put him back and let him grow. They all have them. Our Husky said he had only two-a male and female-but they had children. Eskimo baby is in hood on back. Wears only coat with hood. Against mother's bare back. Doctor [Cook] was taking picture of mother and she seemed very nervous. After picture, took baby out and held him over a tin can. Later the baby joed on mama's back. She stripped to waist on deck and other woman washed her.

—Wyckoff

SUNDAY, AUGUST 4TH, 1901

Up at 8:30 A.M. Very rough night in Smith Sound. Found everything moveable on cabin floor. On account of imperfect charts and ice, we passed Etah [by] 20 miles. Now on way back. Ice on all sides and hemmed in. Cook, Bridgman, Wyckoff, Church and the Husky [Kaiotah] went ashore to a little settlement of Eskimos in distance for news and our position. They had a hard time keeping off the ice. Dr. Cook gave the Huskies a bath this morning. Used corrosive supplement to get rid of the bugs.

This is an off day. Everything has gone wrong about the ship. Officers and crew grumbling at the slightest thing. We in the cabin feeling fine; all had a good night's rest. We found out that we had gone fully 20 miles beyond Etah. Took on four more Huskies and got into Etah at 6 P.M. Found the

Windward with Mr. and Mrs. Peary and little girl [Marie Peary] who looks like Ariel.[95] Also Dr. Dedrick. Found everybody well and on the lookout for us. We saw them first and blew the whistle. They came over to supper.

This is a fjord, a medium-sized glacier at the end, high banks covered with green moss at the bottom, with a dark shade of hilltop above the dark red earth. Then at [the] top, black. Saw millions of little auks.[96] Peary is about 5 foot 10 inches, broad across the shoulders, sandy complexion, [and] very ordinary-looking man and very much stuck on himself. Mrs. Peary is tall, slim, attractive face, not pretty, but interesting and sociable. We spent the balance of August hunting walrus, deer, and all game, to supply Peary with food for another winter as he intends to stay and make his final dash [for the North Pole]. Mrs. Peary and girl come home with us. Stein[97] and Warmbath[98] are down to North Humberland Island. We expect to get them on our way down. We made 78° 30' latitude today.

—Bement

Went past Etah as far as Cairn Point. When our Eskimo, Kiota, came on deck he recognized the country and was very much excited; said we were all dumb, so we turned back. On the way south, Kiota discovered an Eskimo village which, he said, was called Anoratuk.

95. Bement's ten-year-old daughter.

96. Any of several usually black and white diving birds of the family Alcidae, of northern seas, having webbed feet and small wings; most Inuit wore a shirt made from 75–100 skins of the auk.

97. An American geologist from Washington, D.C., who visited

Greenland with Peary in 1897 and returned on the *Erik* in 1901, today Robert Stein is considered the first real enthusiast to study Inuit songs.

98. William Warmbath, of Boston, Massachusetts, served as Robert Stein's assistant.

Dr. Cook cleaning (W35/B96)

Marie Ahnighito Peary (W43/B48)

"Dear little snow baby! How we all loved her, no wonder the Eskimo women came from all around to see her and give her presents." (Kersting, The White World, *172*)

OPPOSITE: **The Pearys with Professor Limond Stone** (W117) FAC

Kaiotah (B303)

"...there was no one on board who knew anything about our where-abouts, so we ran by and on into Kane Basin, and I think if it had not been for an Eskimo [Kaiotah] we had picked up at Cape York we would have made the Pole." (Wyckoff Notes)

Church and I rowed Mr. Bridgman, the doctor [Cook] and the Husky ashore. We found that we were up against a very strong head wind and tide; with a bungling fleet to man the skiff, we barely moved. This was the worst rowing I have ever undertaken, and if we had any distance to go we could not possibly have made it. On shore we found the Eskimos living in skin tents and stone houses. The tents being the summer habitation, and the stone houses or igloos for permanent winter quarters. We found that the snow igloo, which is generally pictured as a habitation of the Eskimo, was only resorted to when traveling in the winter months, and only then as a temporary shelter.

All about us was much evidence of game—bear, deer, musk ox, walrus, narwhal, seal, white and blue fox, hare and birds. Mr. Bridgman and the doctor [Cook] did some trading with the Eskimos, and got everything that was of any use or value as souvenirs. On the way back, Mr. Bridgman allowed four more Huskies to get into the boat with us and would have allowed more except that there was not even standing room. We had nine in a boat that should have accommodated not more than three people, and I for one, hardly expected to make the Erik in the strong tide that was running. *Expected we would all drown in small boat.* Some way we managed to get aboard, I never quite knew how, and it was simply a piece of good luck, which happily balanced poor management.

The new Huskies informed us that Peary and the Windward were at Etah and we immediately got under way for that point. Arrived at Etah a couple of hours later and found everyone alive and well. The Windward had been frozen in at Cape Sabine

Sewing skins (B293)

Inuit women teach Marie Ahnighito to sew garments.

A quiet talk (B50/W93)

Mrs. Josephine Peary speaks privately with Dr. Frederick Cook.

where Peary had found her sometime in May. The Windward had been frozen into the ice voluntarily because during the previous summer they found no trace of Peary. As a matter of fact, he [Peary] summered at Fort Conger three or four hundred miles north of Cape Sabine, and only came south *in May* when the winter made traveling possible along the ice afoot. Dr. Dedrick, Matthew Henson, the colored man, returned with Mr. Peary. Stein and Warmbath wintered at Cape Sabine near the Windward and they are now at Northumberland Island waiting to be picked up on our way home.

After anchor went down, Bridgman and Dr. Cook went over to the Windward alone. Peary with his wife and daughter, Captain Samuel Bartlett, and Dr. Dedrick, came to dinner. Met them but could get no news. Louis, Berri, and I had to wait for third table. *We got no news; nor have we any at midnight. All is very secret. Poor repayment for my five thousand dollars.[99] Think it is damn rotten that I was left out of everything. Will pay rest of five and resign from Club. Bridgman forgot to mention I was member of Club.[100]* We have had absolutely no information as to the success or failure of Peary's expedition. The only information we have gotten has been what we have seen: they are all here and alive. I cannot understand this secrecy especially as I did my share toward bringing the expedition up here.

Dedrick was as dirty as Huskies. Didn't get chance to examine others.

—Wyckoff

MONDAY, AUGUST 5TH, 1901

Up at 6:30 A.M. On the way to the auk rookeries at 7:30 A.M. (Church, Wyckoff, Berri, Stone, four Huskies, and myself). The rookeries are rocks that have fallen down from the high cliffs and lodged on top of each other leaving small holes between them where they [auks] build their nests.[101] They roost on these rocks by the millions. At first we shot them on the wing, but that was too hard work. So [we] sat down among the rocks and waited for them to settle. Then each one picked out a bunch and fired at a given signal. Wyckoff killed the most in one shot (12). We got 150 birds and stopped in about one hour's time. They are about the size of a small pigeon and fine eating. The doctor [Cook] took the boat and went up to photograph a glacier about 5 miles off. Did not get back until 2 o'clock and we were tired, cold, [and] hungry, to say nothing of being cross. He had two kunas[102] and three mickininnies more with him. Back to ship at 3 P.M. Had lunch; then went Arctic hare hunting. Walked about 8 miles over rocks; roughest journey I ever had. Wyckoff and Church went back to the ship, had an engagement to dine with Peary. I continued hunting. Shot one hare. [Then I] got caught in a snow squall; lasted only about 10 minutes, but was fierce. Got on the lee side of a rock until [it was] over, then made for the ship. Got aboard at 7:30 P.M. Played chess until 11:30 P.M.

—Bement

99. Wyckoff pledged to the Peary Arctic Club $1000 a year for four years to support Peary in his Arctic work. In addition, he paid $500 each, for himself and Louis Bement, to travel on the *Erik* as guests.

100. *Peary Arctic Club.*
101. Auks lay their eggs among loose rocks without building nests.
102. Word for women in Inuit language.

**Marie Ahnighito attempts to retrieve her rabbit on the
bridge of the *Erik*** (W40/B101)

*"One morning, bright and early, I was awakened by Dad standing
by the side of my bunk, asking me to put my hand into his coat
pocket. I sat up, only half awake, but very curious, and reached
down into the pocket he held out to me. I felt something warm
and soft and furry and drawing my hand out very gently, found
that I was holding the fattest little rabbit that I had ever
seen."[Marie Ahnighito Peary,* The Snowbaby's Own Story
(New York: Frederick A. Stokes, 1934), 126]

Started early to shoot little auks. Went to luminary near Etah and found millions of birds. Shot many on the wing, but they would fall in rocks and we could not find them. But undoubtedly, if we waited, they would settle all around us and then we could get them in bunches. Think I killed fully 150. Bement and I killed 23 in one shot. While we were shooting, Dr. Cook took the boat and Husky oars and went away for a half hour. After we had expended all of our ammunition, we settled down to wait [for] the doctor's return. Had to wait for him four hours—his half hour was really about eight—and this is about as near the doctor gets to anything. *New spell; damn the doctor.*

Late in the afternoon went out after Arctic hare, but they were evidently pretty well hunted out before we arrived. Bement shot one. Had rather a dangerous trip of it altogether as we were obliged to climb some rather steep and crumbling cliffs. At one time the Captain, who was along, thought I was gone *because he called to Louis to go back.*

In the evening I was invited with one other (Louis and Fred matched and Fred went) to dinner on the Windward. We obtained no news. Mr. and Mrs. Peary seemed very pleasant. We had a good dinner. They seem to live on the Windward after the twelve months in the ice fully as well if not better than we do on the Erik. The dinner was really quite an event, as we had to get into our good clothes.

—Wyckoff

Robert Peary coming up the companionway (B102/W37)

TUESDAY, AUGUST 6TH, 1901

Up at 8 A.M. Mr. and Mrs. Peary and Marie came aboard with their possessions and at 10:15 weighed anchor and started south for Engelfield Gulf to hunt walrus and deer. Long talk with Peary today. Stopped at Nerkee[103] [and] took on Matt [Henson] and two Huskies. Made bunk for them in hold.[104]

Anchored in Robertson Bay with Hakluyt [Island] and Cumberland [sic] Island in full view. Anchored near a glacier, estimated it about anywhere from 500 feet to one mile. Started at 10 P.M. Fairly well bundled. Went about one half mile. We commenced to take off our heavy clothing, stacked them, and went on stripped down to shirtsleeves. All carried guns. Got one shot at eider duck. Found glacier fully three miles from ship. We started to climb but had to cut steps in the side with our ice axes. Reached the top after an hour's hard work. We named it "Bum Glacier." The fun commenced when we started down. Only had two ice axes and no rope. Stone went ahead and cut deeper steps and all went well until we were in about twenty feet from the part where the snow left off. Then it was so steep that we simply fell that distance in the snow. None of us were hurt, and when we reached bottom, considered it great fun. When we got back to the boat, found the tide had come in about 12 feet. Boat floating out to sea. We fortunately had enough to stretch a rope about 40 feet, and put big strain on it. [We] had to wade into our boot tops to get the painter.[105] Found another Husky ashore and

took him on board. Arrived on ship at 1:30 A.M. We hunted up everything we could, to eat; found oranges, bananas, candy, cheese, and onions. Sat on deck until 2:15 A.M., then went to bed.
—Bement

Mr. and Mrs. Peary and Marie came on board today to remain with us for our stay up here. The Erik is more commodious and a more powerful boat than the Windward, and Peary thinks he can get about better and faster on our boat. Mr. Peary and family have taken Mr. Bridgman's stateroom and Mr. Bridgman has taken Church's. He has moved into a cubbyhole back over the propeller. Took on Matt Henson at one of the native settlements.

We have started on a three days hunt for walrus, but have gotten none today. We anchored for the night near Red Clift where Mr. Peary wintered sometime ago. We stopped during the day quite near the site of the Red Clift House and all hands went ashore to examine the ruins; absolutely nothing remains as the Huskies carried off every particle of wood and metal. Even an old nail is too precious to lose in this country.

Our final anchorage was opposite a glacier, which ended inland, apparently a short walk. We five youngsters[106] thought we would examine the glacier and eventually got to it, although we found that it really ended several miles inland. We found a place where we could climb the side with the use of the two ice axes that we carried. It was very steep and

---

103. Means meat in Inuit language and was an Inuit settlement sixty miles by sledge south of Etah on Inglefield Bay.
104. The entire cargo space in the hull of a vessel between the

lowermost deck and the bottom.
105. Bow rope.
106. Probably referring to Bement, Berri, Stone, Church, and himself.

Afternoon at the wheel (W94/B58)

*l. to r. Mrs. Charles Percy, George Wardwell, Marie Ahnighito Peary
(within wheel spokes), Fred Church, Louis Bement (at wheel), and
Professor Stone (right).*

Matthew Henson (right) with unknown sailor at the
wheel (W72)

Matthew Henson (W73/B55)

Sitting in front of winches that carry loads on and off the ship.

Collecting relics (W127/B51)

*Peary speaks to Bridgman at site of Red Cliff House while Bement
(center) and Josephine Peary (right) look on. Fred Church (front)
searches for anything remaining from the old house.*

we made our ascent only by means of steps chopped in the ice. The surface of the glacier was running with water as the ice seemed to be melting very rapidly; quite a stream flowed from the base. We went up the glacier quite a distance and on our return found that our steps were pretty well melted and after a thorough examination found that there was no way to get off without taking a good sixty to eighty foot slide. This was rather disagreeable on account of the water, but we all made it, landing safely in a snowdrift at the foot. *Got back at 1:15 A.M.* —Wyckoff

WEDNESDAY, AUGUST 7TH, 1901

Up at 8 A.M. Sighted walruses in about one hour. Wyckoff and Church, with a boatload of Huskies, started after them. They worked through the ice for about one half hour. Then we saw that they had fired, and saw the Huskies throw their harpoons. They signaled us, and the ship started at once for them.

When we arrived, found they had shot a big cow and her calf. [The] estimated weight of cow: 2000 lbs; [the] calf: 400 pounds, and only two weeks old. They have about as much shape as a _____.[107] They cut a slit in back of [its] neck, about three inches wide, and put a hook in [the] slit, and hauled one ton of flesh aboard. They were curiosities to us and everybody examined them very closely. Eleven feet long; [possibly] ten feet. Hauled both up and in about one half hour, sighted another. Church, Stone, Berri, and myself wanted one this time. We rode

within twenty feet of them; saw four on the pan. Each was to take one but could not get a shot at two; so Stone and I turned on the other two and we all fired at once. Two were killed outright, one slipped off the pan, and one of the Huskies harpooned him just as he was about disappearing. They also shot one in the end on the pan, so if he slipped off, the float would hold him up. In about a minute, twelve walruses appeared and all made a rush for the boat. They made things lively for us. One came up and hit the boat. I fired at him and drove him off; but back they came with a rush. I got the walrus fever and pumped a shell through my gun. The others had more or less the same experience. We drove them off about fifty feet and for twenty minutes kept firing. Hit a lot of them. But if killed in the water with air out of their lungs, they sank, so we only got two. Each weighed about a ton each. We got six the first day. —Bement

Spent the day shooting walrus. Church and I shooting the first one. During the day we got several but found that our 30-40 Winchesters had little effect unless the first shot struck a vital spot. The herd of walrus that we were in is a cowherd. It seems that at this time of year cows and their calves separate from the bulls, the cowherd keeping to this section of Whale Sound, and the bull herd in Wostenholm Sound. The cows average from 1100 to 2000 pounds in weight, while the bulls go as high as two tons in weight.

107. Bement may have intended to fill in the blank later.

Looking for walruses (W 106)

*l. to r. Moses Bartlett, Dr. Frederick Cook, and Robert Peary
(with binoculars).*

Inuk about to harpoon a walrus (B329) FAC

"It is rather difficult to find the vital spot for shooting a walrus and unless you find it, even a 30–40 mushroom bullet will make no impression on the immense bulk of the animal. The surest way to get your game is to get near enough so that an Eskimo can get his harpoon into one." (Wyckoff Notes)

Matthew Henson demonstrates the Inuit method of hunting (B325)

Leaning out over the boat, Henson is ready to harpoon a walrus while an Inuk looks on.

Walrus hunting in Whale Sound (B198)
The men work as a team to haul a walrus onto the ship.

The Eskimo method of capturing the walrus seems the most effective. A sharp watch is kept from the loft and when one or more walrus are sighted sleeping on a pan of ice the ship is stopped and the shooting party takes to the whaleboat. We usually send out two or three of our party with guns. Have Eskimo rowers and an Eskimo harpoon thrower; Matt or Dr. Dedrick take charge of the boat.

The walrus come up on the ice to sleep and it is necessary to come up upon them quietly so that we can get within harpoon throwing distance before they are aware of our presence. When striking distance is reached the Eskimo throws his harpoon, which is attached by a twenty foot walrus hide rope to a float made from the skin of a seal. After the harpoon has been planted in the walrus's body, we alleged hunters attempt to kill him with the guns. The vital spot is located somewhere in the neighborhood of the shoulder. Unless hit in the vital spot bullets seem to make no impression, and it usually takes from ten to twenty shots to bag our game. Occasionally we have attempted to shoot first and throw the harpoon afterwards, but generally [it] results in the walrus escaping. Even when the walrus has been mortally wounded, they [*sic*] will sometimes slip off the pan and sink to the bottom, so where possible we stick to the Husky method. —Wyckoff

THURSDAY, AUGUST 8TH, 1901
Up at 8:30 A.M. On the outlook for walrus. Sighted some and lowered boat. Got two. Did not go on next boatload. They got two. Sighted one single one on pan. I went alone with the Huskies, rode up within 35 feet. He awoke and I shot him over

Skinning and cutting a walrus (B80)

Moses Bartlett, First Mate of Erik, *and Matthew Henson watch
Inuk skin and cut up a walrus.*

flipper. Off the pan he went. Came up within 15 feet of boat. Husky harpooned him and held on the line; and we had a ride for about 100 feet. He came up in direct rays of the sun and I shot, missed him; down he went. He touched us again for about 50 feet and when he came up, shot him through the brain, which settled him. The ship came up head on [toward] us. The engine refused to reverse and they just hurried us by going to port, which threw the stern about on us. But by good oarsmanship, [we] got out of the way [of the ship]. This [was] the fourth time such a thing had happened to us. Made up my mind not to go again unless the ship is at anchor. Struck a herd of about fifty. Shot at them from the bow of ship. Seven of us used 160 cartridges. Killed three we know of. Got 12, all told, in 2 days. On the outlook for the Windward. Wyckoff, Church, Berri, and myself going to Olrik Bay for 10 days, deer hunting. Go out camping. Got great outfit. Did not find the Windward at Nerki. Anchored overnight. Got our trip together.
—Bement

Still after walrus. Did bum shooting—think I killed about one and am ashamed to say how many I shot at. Bagged total of nine for the day. *Church and self shot two others later: a fine bull. [On second thought] must have been a female as bulls all go together in separate herd down in Wostenholm Sound.* The Eskimos cut up the game on deck and the ship looks like a slaughterhouse. As the ship moves along, you can see a red trail behind us for miles.

  While Church and I were out on the ice one time, the captain nosed into the floe so that we could get aboard without sending a boat out for us.

His method was to ram full speed and as the ship came where we had been standing we were obliged to run for our lives.

At another time when Church, Bement, Berri and Stone were out with Matt in the whale boat, they shot three walrus; two were killed at the pan where they were sleeping, the third had been harpooned and was held up by the float. The Erik had stopped about a mile away and after the shooting the captain decided to run up alongside the pan and take party and game aboard. He ran toward the pan full speed until he was within about one hundred yards, [and] then signaled to reverse the engines. As our boat is very bulky and the engines very small, reverse at full speed makes little difference in the headway of the boat. The captain realized that we could not stop until we had passed the pan a long distance and so shouted to the helmsman to put her over hard a starboard. I was on the bridge at the time and saw that he did not realize that with the propeller reversed, his order should have been hard a port; as it was we immediately began to swing in toward the pan. There was hardly time to do anything and I shouted to the captain to reverse his engines sending her full speed ahead, realizing that this would swing her off from the pan. The captain seemed absolutely stupefied; could not size up the condition; could not understand why we were swinging down on the boat, which had been partially drawn up on the pan. I did not think he heard me shout or at least realized my meaning, but I saw that something had to be done, and done quickly, for if our boat ever touched that pan of ice everybody would have been overboard and in water of a temperature of

28°F. There was absolutely no hope for any of the party. I shouted to him again and started for the signal levers to give him my order personally, but just as I reached him he evidently came to enough to follow instructions, for he gave the engineer the signal and we passed by the pan with only about six feet to spare. Matt was so excited he could talk only Husky, and the whole party were [*sic*] as white as snow. Even after we began to swing away from them there was danger that they would be sucked into the propeller and for a few minutes the situation looked absolutely hopeless. We passed them by and the captain brought about the ship [and] came to sufficiently far away from them that time. When the party arrived on board most of them were trembling still with the excitement.

Another instance of the captain's management was when Church and I were out in the boat with a Husky crew; he came so near running us down that we could have touched the boat as she went by us. If the Huskies had not fended off with their oars and backed water we could have had at least a serious accident.

From conversations with the captain we have been able to get a little of his history, and it is only surprising that we have escaped serious trouble many times before. At one time, evidently, a good many years ago, the captain was a pilot in the Canadian Government employ. He wrecked his vessel; he was thrown out of the service; he took up his old job of house painting and had been so employed up to the time he arranged to go with us. I would rather trust a boat like the Erik in the hands of any land lubber who has common sense, then to put it in charge of the captain, for he has

Captain Blakeney (W69)
"Our captain, a Mr. Blakeney, was a house painter by trade, but at one time had been employed on a ship in some capacity or other." (Wyckoff Notes)

Fullerton, Chief Engineer, behind hatch cover (W68)

*"The engineer is a Scotchman and a good fellow and apparently
competent, but his engines are of the vintage of '76 and he is
naturally handicapped." (Wyckoff Diary)*

not even common sense. The whole outfit, however, is about on a par with the captain.

Mr. Bridgman, the commander of our expedition, is a busy man so he left the arrangement of details to Captain Farquhar of Halifax, the owner of the Erik. He could not arrange a summer picnic for me. He engaged the captain and all of the crew. The first and second officers are New Foundlanders and they are the best of the lot with the exception possibly of the engineer. They have been brought up on sailing vessels and know more or less of the sea, but neither of them, as far as I can learn, has had even a common school education, and neither of them knows anything about navigating a ship except what they have picked up before the mast. The first mate was drunk the day we came aboard the ship and was ordering the captain all about and was laying down the law on all points and the captain took it. The engineer is a Scotchman and a good fellow and apparently competent, but his engines are of the vintage of '76 and he is naturally handicapped.
—Wyckoff

FRIDAY, AUGUST 9TH, 1901
Up at 8:15 A.M. Everything ready for trip. Looking for the Windward. Ran into a herd of walruses. Shot at them from the bow of the Erik. Killed three. Got one aboard. Sighted the Windward at 3 P.M. Aboard Windward at 5 P.M. Started for Stein and Warmbath camp at Cape Josephine Head, North Humberland Island. Church, Wyckoff, Berri, Bridgman, and myself went ashore. Warmbath met us on the beach. Stein soon arrived; delivered mail to them. [Samuel] Warmbath looks like

Deck of *Erik* loaded with walrus meat (B163)
"No musk oxen, boat loads of ducks, plenty of seal and for walrus, we brought them in by the ton to be used for both man and dog food." (Bement Notes)

Inuk cutting up walrus on deck lined with carcasses (B160)

"Altogether we killed 78 walrus and as these averaged in weight from a ton to two tons we had quite a cargo. The deck was over-run and only enough space left for a narrow passageway. A good deal of the flesh had to be thrown into the hold." (Wyckoff Notes)

Paderewski;[108] long hair, very black, dark complexion, smooth face, medium height, large nose. Stein looks like Professor Short. Very high forehead, full beard, wears glasses. Both looked very shabby. [Their] camp [consisted of] 2 tents [with] bird, fox, hare, [and] skins all about camp drying. Used auk skins instead of paper (discovered by Wyckoff). Back to ship at 2 A.M. Cut up 15 walruses today on deck of Windward. The bloodiest and [most] stinking mess I ever saw or want for. Impossible to walk aft, except over walrus, or parts of walrus. Anchor up at 6 A.M. Landed at Red Cliff, Peary's old quarters. Look over the site of the house; pick up relics, sighted white whales. Clarence and I took some shots of them. Each hit them, [but] did not kill any. Looked as white as snow in the water.
—Bement

Went on board the Windward with Church, Bement, Berri, and Bridgman. The Erik is to go to Cape York and return, stopping at all native settlements for trading purposes. Will be gone about ten days. We on the Windward go to Olrick's Bay for deer, stopping first at Northumberland *Island* to *give* ultimatum to Stein and Warmbath. It seems they came up here to explore west coast of Ellesmere Land. Stayed two years and did nothing but gather a few specimens. These must go to Arctic Club or they can not go home. Also they must agree to pay for provisions they have had from Windward: about $70.00 worth.

108. A Polish pianist, composer, patriot and statesman, 1860–1941.

Arrived at Cape Josephine Head and landed at their camp. It was a wreck and so were Stein and Warmbath. When they came north they had practically no knowledge of fieldwork and brought very little with them in the way of food and camp equipment. Five pounds of tea was their two years' supply and everything else in about the same proportion. What little they did bring was used up long ago, and if it had not been for the Windward and the Eskimos they would have undoubtedly starved. Their tent was in rags and repaired with fur. At times they have had to act as tent poles to keep it from blowing away. Neither had hats—long hair—very ragged clothing, partially fur. *They* agreed to anything if we would take them home. Seemed very glad to go. Left them until we returned. I attempted to be nice to Stein and was ready and willing to give him any information as regards current history, but he did not seem interested. He asked me if I had met so-and-so, Eskimo friends of his, and did not I think they had an unusual amount of grass, and was not the view grand. Had evidently lost all interest in everything except his Eskimo life.
—Wyckoff

SATURDAY, AUGUST 10TH, 1901
Cold and raw; rain this morning. Up at 8 A.M. All eat forward. Berri and I slept in the Erie R.R. caboose[109] on benches. Wyckoff and Church slept aft in cabin on seats. Stayed all day in caboose, smoking and listening to accounts of the north from Dr. Dedrick and Captain Bartlett (who by the way looks exactly like Father Taber).[110] This boat makes 3 miles per hour under favorable circumstances under steam; possible to cut out 10 or more under sail. We run into strong blow at 12:00 noon. Did not move an inch until sail was set. Anchored at 6 P.M. Too much ice and wind. Heavy snowstorm at 9 P.M. Church and Berri just brought in two Arctic hare. Four meals a day on the Windward: 8 A.M., 12 P.M., 6 P.M., and 10 P.M. and more if you wish it.
—Bement

En route to Olrick Bay. *Had to anchor.* Had [an anchor] leeward of Herbert Island as we had a head wind. The Windward cannot make headway against a fair breeze.

Am getting acquainted with Dr. Dedrick and Captain Sam Bartlett. Captain Sam wears a smile and a stiff short right leg; looks sleepy but is well-read and very wide-awake if there is anything doing. Knows where most of the rocks are around the Pole. Has struck most of them. Windward goes so slow she doesn't knock paint off when she hits.
—Wyckoff

SUNDAY, AUGUST 11TH, 1901
Turned in last night at 12:30. Up at 11:30 A.M. Still at anchor. Strong gale all night with heavy snowstorm. Arctic hare and eider duck for dinner; fine plum duff. Everybody in Erie R.R. today listening

109. An old railroad caboose was placed on the deck of the *Windward* as a cabin.

110. Probably referring to his father-in-law, whose surname was Taber.

Samuel Bartlett, Captain of *Windward* (B40)

"The handling of a ship in the ice pack where the tides are so strong is a beautiful and thrilling piece of work and Captain Sam Bartlett was a past master. A ship has about as much chance as that snowball we have heard so much about." (Bement Notes)

Deck gear on the Windward (B167)

to Dr. Dedrick's experiences. Very interesting. Discussed Stein's Eskimo vocabulary and had a Husky as interpreter. All agreed that it is not a standard morning.

—Bement

Still anchored *in bay, Northumberland Island*. Wind is still in the same direction.

—Wyckoff

MONDAY, AUGUST 12TH, 1901

Up at 7:30 A.M. Under way at 6:00 A.M. Sun shining; looks like a spring morning. After two days and nights of rain, snow, and heavy gales, seems like the sun [went] south. At 3:30 P.M., entered Olrick Bay. Spent morning in Erie R.R. swapping lies, and smoking. Eastern end of Herbert Island looks like cloth draped over the earth, shading from fawn to brown. Anchored at 8 P.M. upper Narrows.

—Bement

Lifted anchor. Arrived in Olricks Bay. Wind shifted and we have gotten as far as the mouth of Salmon River about halfway up Olricks Bay.

We are anchored again as the tide is going out.

—Wyckoff

TUESDAY, AUGUST 13TH, 1901

Up at 7:30 A.M. Started after deer at 8:30. Sighted one on the beach. Church, Wyckoff, Berri, Dr. [Dedrick], and myself went with a Husky each for guide. Berri and I landed for deer. Wind shifts. We were to the windward. Deer scented us and it was all up. Started back up valley and all separated. My guide took me back about 5 miles over what I

thought a rough land, but changed my mind later. We started up a ravine, the rockiest road ever traveled over. Had to climb up the rocks like the side of a house. Got up at last and just sat down and a deer appeared. I shot first and missed. Husky shot and hit him in flank. I shot twice more; all went about a foot over his neck. Husky ran over the rocks where he got two more shots. One hit him just behind the ear and settled him. We started to skin him and got skin almost off when Berri and Husky came in sight. Just then, another deer appeared at 600 yards. I shot three times and every shot went directly over his back. Berri shot ten times. None hit. Mister deer got away. Berri after him. We got deer cut up and cached him and started out again. Walked steady for 4 hours and never saw a deer. Climbed mountains of rocks, elevation of fully 1800 feet. Started back at 5 P.M. from where we cached the deer and the Husky tied a rope around the meat and with rope over his head, packed the 100 pounds of meat back to ship. Five hour walk over rocks, down gorges, with five rests. Back at 10 P.M. Dr. [Dedrick] had arrived with three hare. Berri came in next at 11 P.M.; no game. Wyckoff next [at] 12:00 P.M.; no game. Church next with one deer. One Husky stayed out all night; went to tea at 3:00 A.M. I packed in deerskin last mile. Could hardly walk my feet troubled me so; never suffered such agony before with my feet. Estimated walk: 20 miles, equal to 40 over good country; elevation 2000 feet. Husky's name [is] Penlov [Pooblah].

—Bement

Anchored off *camp river* (Hawk Mountain) and there was great excitement as two reindeer had

Pooblah (B302)

Louis Bement's guide on deer hunt.

been sighted. The Huskies sighted them first and pointed them out with cries of "tucktoo[III] matluck tucktoo." Berri and a Husky started after the two first seen and the rest of us prepared for a more extensive trip inland.

The country at this point is bold and mountainous and almost bare of snow and ice for 18 to 20 miles inland. The shores rise up so abruptly in most places as to make traveling all but impossible. There is a small stream, which comes down north of Hawk Mountain, and we are going to try up this valley for deer.

The doctor [Dedrick], two Huskies and myself started up the left side of the valley, the rest of the party taking the right, and such a scrambling as it was. Nothing as far as the eye could see but boulders—boulders of all sizes and all shapes—heaped up as if by the evil one himself to prevent our progress. After about four miles of this, and when I was beginning to believe that deer hunting was not the greatest of pleasure, we were stopped by one of the Eskimos. He claimed he saw deer and pointed to a mountain three or four miles off to prove it. I had to take his word for it for even with the aid of the field glasses I could make nothing out. My companion finally thought he saw something move and we decided to separate, he to make for a promising looking valley that had been to our left and I with my Husky guide for the alleged deer. By this time we were pretty well up on the mountainside and had to make down across the valley and part way up the mountain to the other side. How we

got down that mountain without breaking our necks is more than I know. It is a wonderful thing to see one of those natives jumping along from rock to rock and at breakneck speed, but some way he did it, and more wonderful to me, I was close after him. The scent of game was in the air and I had forgotten that I really did not care much for deer hunting. We made along the bed of the stream until we came opposite where the deer had been seen and then began our climb. Stooping, creeping, crawling, we made our way for Cawingwah, who made us understand that we were in the neighborhood of our game. After about 3/4 of a mile of this kind of going I heard a grunt from the Husky and looked around and there were our deer. They had been traveling also and had worked so far down that we had almost passed them, and stood there, feet braced and heads thrown back staring at the strange intruders. It was as pretty a sight as I have ever witnessed. There were three of them, a buck, a doe, and a fawn, apparently taken bodily from some old picture of Santa Claus and his deer. Cawingwah was nudging me and calling to shake her up and shoot, but I could not, it was too pretty a sight to spoil and I simply stood and watched them as they finally turned and bounded off up the mountainside, stopping every now and again to look back at the disturbers of their eternal quiet. Two or three times I raised my gun to my shoulder and started to press the trigger but I could not bring myself to do it.

During the day I saw altogether 18 deer and shot at one but missed. My Eskimo guide was a boy and

III. Inuit word for caribou.

Deer hunting adventure in Hawk Mountain (B85)

l. to r. Berri, Wyckoff, Dedrick, and Bement. "In this section as we learned from the Eskimo, there were many deer. The hills were indented with valleys where the sun, shining twenty-four hours a day, warmed the meager soil, permitting moss and grass, and even some flowers to mature." (Clarence Wyckoff, "A Caribou Hunt on Peary's 1898–1902 Expedition," Arctic 5 no. 3, 1952: 178)

Meal time on deer hunt (C7)

*l. to r. Berri, Dedrick, Wyckoff, Church, with Inuk in background.
"Finally I sat down with them, cut a strip of meat from the deer's hind
quarter, and gingerly tasted it. It was delicious. That was one of the best
meals I ever had. As a wind-up an Eskimo would cut out a bone, crack
it between two stones, and with a thumb extract the marrow. I tried that
also and it proved a fitting dessert to a wonderful meal." (Wyckoff, "A
Caribou Hunt on Peary's 1898–1902 Expedition," 182)*

Mahhotcher "Mud puddle" (left) and
Kahrashoo (right) standing in front
of the Erie Railroad caboose (B298)

really of very little use. Formerly the deer were easy to get, but now run at sight or smell. *Run always and then stop to look.*

Walked altogether about 40 miles. Church shot two deer. *One ran and was found two days later by doctor [Dedrick] and myself. We ate part of it.*
—Wyckoff

WEDNESDAY, AUGUST 14TH, 1901
Up at 9 A.M. Sore all over. Hardly walk. Went about deck for an hour and limbered up. Had dinner of venison and hare, [known as] Red Cliff stew. Started out at 2 P.M. with Wyckoff. Took new route. Supposed to be shortcut to deer country. Stopped at 4 P.M., had lunch, went to sleep on the rocks (1400 feet up; very warm). Sun got behind mountain peak and we awoke nearly frozen. Started up again. Reached top. Had to take new route down. Hardest coming down yet on account of sore feet and corns. Did not see a deer shot at since. Have long distances. Wyckoff nearly caught one in his hands. Hit one with a rock so thick that we kicked them out of our way. Back to the ship at 11 A.M. All in, but better condition than the day before. Decided to take tent and camp in five miles so as to save us a 10-mile tramp every day. So, got under our packs ready for tomorrow. Four more Huskies came aboard. Came from nobody knows where. Two are old men. One name sounds like Aqua Mud Puddle. So we call him Mud Puddle for short. New ice is forming in the sound but do not feel the cold at all. Seems like weather at home; about 80°F or more.
—Bement

Started with Bement for big lake valley (where Church shot deer and where I had seen a number of mine). Took a shortcut around Hawk Mountain. Found the pass was almost a mountain in itself. Kept climbing and at about 1:00 P.M. arrived at top of pass only to find that it did not lead to the valley at all, but back to the bay. Had to go back and it took us until 11:00 P.M. to get to the ship. Saw no deer. Shortcuts in the Arctic are a delusion and a snare. The doctor [Cook] and Peary both say so. The air is so clear you can form no idea of distance and everything is generally distorted.

During the day we lay down and went to sleep, and slept until the sun went behind a mountain and then we woke up very cold.
—Wyckoff

THURSDAY, AUGUST 15TH, 1901
Up at 7:30. All in good condition, except poor Berri who can hardly walk. Have everything ready to pack in my load; weighs fully fifty pounds, exclusive of gun. Five-mile pack. Start made at 11 A.M. Everybody stripped down to thinnest clothing and suffering at that. Reached camping spot at 2:30 P.M. Everybody all in. Got tent up; fireplace built. Started discussions, through at 6 P.M. Rested, and Church, Berri, and myself started out after deer at 7 P.M. Went 6 miles back over mountains. Church took trail over [a] second mountain. Berri and I took valley pass. We startled a fawn. Both shot, but missed. He started down mountain to two deer. Middow[112] took shot at long range. Both missed. Tried to drive him over to Church. Berri chased

112. Bement's Inuit guide.

Inuit camp (B304) FAC

Woman and children at camp (B312) FAC

"The Eskimo are, generally speaking, an industrious people, healthy and
strong, harmless, kindhearted, very mirthful and rather good-looking, the
children being always pretty and some of the maidens beautiful."
(Kersting, The White World, *124)*

him all over meadow, like chasing a calf. Could not get him to lie down. Fawn made circle and got away in mountains. Met Church at appointed place. Went over to big lake and then started back to camp over new pass (describe pass). Reached camp; all in got supper of venison, hare, tea, coffee, bacon, cake, etc. Church and I made a milk punch out of condensed milk. Great; recommended it to everybody. Sun went back of mountains and got very cold. Water froze 1/4 inch thick in water pail. Got into sleeping bag; all things on but boots. Everybody asleep by 2 A.M.
—Bement

At my suggestion we camped out about four miles up the stream. Packed up over the worst mossy portage I ever saw. Fell twice. Burt,[113] as usual, had more stuff than anyone and made Husky carry it. He is a youth nineteen years old and knows it all. As a matter of fact knows little and we are endeavoring to impress that fact upon him. Jollied him into carrying pack back to ship on return and think it did him good. [He] wanted to cook one day and we would not allow it. Let him make coffee; served same after we went to bed.
—Wyckoff

FRIDAY, AUGUST 16TH, 1901
Up at 12 noon. Was forced up. Everybody asleep. I washed up the dishes from last night's dinner. Everybody got up. None of us could move. Feet sore

and muscles all drawn up. Got dinner by 1:30 P.M. All decided to stay in camp. Played pitching quoits[114] with towel and kunas.[115] Duck on the rock and resting. Laying out our trip for tomorrow. Found a dead deer that Church had shot the day before. Supper at 7 P.M.: Danish. Had fried potatoes, fried sardines, figs, candy, bread, ship biscuits, bacon, [and] imperial cheese. Saw baby Husky eating raw meat with knife; age 3. Wyckoff and Church [did the cooking]. Berri, and I [were the] dishwashers. Doctor [Dedrick] general superintendent. Huskies on watch. Two kunas, two kids came into camp today with tupik[116] and set up near us. Even though we are foot-sore and tired, we are having great time and fun.
—Bement

SATURDAY, AUGUST 17TH, 1901
Up at 7:40. Church and Wyckoff started out for deer at 4 A.M. The doctor [Dedrick] went to the ship and all the Huskies were out, making in all about 14. Berri and I got our breakfast at 8:40. Started out we made about 15 mile tramp over the mountain, but saw no deer. They have been hunted so much by our party that they have gone way back. Church and Wyckoff have started in for about 35-mile tramp. Their feet are in bad condition and I doubt if they'll make it. Did not sleep well last night. Had a series of dreams and it was very cold. Saw an apparition on my sleeping bag of a dead

---

113. Wyckoff's nickname for Herbert Berri.
114. A game in which rings of rope or flattened metal are thrown at an upright peg, the object being to encircle it or come as close to it as possible.

115. Perhaps with some of the women they were playing a game of pitching a towel over a resting duck.

Inuk woman with child in hood (C55)

"It must be said in their favor, however, that children as well as aged and infirm members of the tribe are well taken care of, and that for the former the parents evince the liveliest affections." (Peary, Northward over the 'Great Ice'*, 496)*

face. [It was] formed, as I afterwards discovered, by the fastener [of the sleeping bag]. Could not just make out whom it was. That has worried me all day. I hope nothing has happened at home. Expect to land in Sydney one month from today.
—Bement

F. [Church] and I, 30 hours.
—Wyckoff

SUNDAY, AUGUST 18TH, 1901
Wyckoff and Church came in at 7 A.M., having been gone 24 hours. Both [were] in fair condition. Dr. [Dedrick] and I got up and got breakfast for them. All crawled into our bags and went to sleep. Awoke at 2 P.M.; had dinner at 3:30. Lay around, told stories until 8 P.M. Shucked camp and started for the ship; arrived at 11 P.M. Charlie[117] [Percy] had supper ready for us. Turned in at 1 A.M. Church and the Captain[118] stayed up and kept up a continuous gab until 4 A.M., so I got but little sleep. Wyckoff and Church did not get any deer. Saw about 25; could not get within range. Wyckoff is in a rage because he did not shoot any deer. [There is] no living with him. Mr. Bridgman started for our camp Friday and while climbing the mountain detached a stone and a large boulder crashed down on his foot bruising it very severely.
—Bement

To ship at 11; out [at] 3
—Wyckoff

117. The steward for the *Windward*.

118. Probably referring to Captain Bartlett.

Forty-two skins (B78)

The result of the caribou hunts near Hawk Mountain.

MONDAY, AUGUST 19TH, 1901

Up at 12 noon. Found that Wyckoff and Huskies had gone after deer at 5 A.M. He is very persistent. Bet Church a dinner that he would shoot one. Everybody lying about ship, taking it easy, and waiting for the hunting party to return so we can meet the Erik and start for Sabine. One Husky has not shown up for five days. After Wyckoff comes in, going to leave two Huskies ashore to wait for lost Huskies. Wyckoff came in at 6:30 P.M. with a fine buck's head, his first deer. He is satisfied now. Been out 12 hours; he is a wreck. Huskies and all have brought in 30 deer in six days. Church, Berri, and myself have been aboard all day loafing.
—Bement

Arrive 6:30
—Wyckoff

TUESDAY, AUGUST 20TH, 1901

Anchor up on Windward at 5 A.M. Down Olricks Bay to meet [the Erik]. The Windward steamed down to meeting place, but Erik was not there. Dropped anchor and sent two Huskies down to communicate with them. Nothing doing aboard. Sleeping and taking things easy. Received word at 4 P.M. that Erik was down the bay so we went down to meet her, ran along side, and latched together at 10 P.M. A big pan of ice struck the ships and the Windward cast off lines and backed out and got away. Our anchor being down in 20 fathoms of water and 60 fathoms of chains out. Tried to lift anchor, but impossible. Backed up and butted ice but could not raise it and the flow forced us on bottom. Got off after a great deal of struggling and

excitement. Still, the anchor held fast and we were forced ashore twice more. Good luck favored us with a mud bottom. We slipped cable anchor and forced our way out of danger and went across the bay and latched to the Windward again. We transferred our trunks and crawled in our bunks, taking off my clothes the first time in 10 days.
—Bement

Met Erik.
—Wyckoff

WEDNESDAY, AUGUST 21ST, 1901

Slept until noon. Much rested; feeling ok. Windward and Erik transferred coal and ballast. We have taken in about 75 tons of rock ballast. At 2 P.M. discovered that we both were aground again. We cut loose and after much excitement and hard trying, got away into deep water. The Windward anchor being down passed through a similar experience to ours of last night. We helped bunt ice to get it away from her cable. Could not stay long as the tide was going out so left her to work her own way out and we started over to pick up our lost anchor and cable after cruising around for hours. We came to anchor at 9 P.M. to wait until the tide carried out the pan ice so we could see the buoy. Windward got off the ground at 7 P.M. and started for Nerkie. The declination of the sun is very marked, getting a little dark after 9 P.M. We should be on our way to Sabine without a waste of time, or our prospects of being frozen in ice [will] be good. Even with all of our exciting times, we are having great sport. The Erik while we were away got 6 deer and 16 bull walrus. Mr. Peary gave us walrus relics. Mr. Peary

Windward (left) and **Erik** lashed together in Olrik Bay (B172) FAC

"That night the ice came in and drove the Erik ashore and she lost her
anchor and 100 fathoms of cable." (Bement Log)

Windward (left) and the *Erik* with two members of the
Windward crew (K2)

had 7 walrus heads cleaned for us and they were all
mixed up so we could not tell whose head
belonged to whom. They were so near alike [that]
we threw dice for choice. Stone 1st, Church and I
tied for 2nd and on "shake off" beat me so I get
3rd, Berri 4th, Dr. Cook 5th, Wyckoff 6th, Goldstein
7th but there is little choice.
—Bement

Shipped cable.
—Wyckoff

THURSDAY, AUGUST 22ND, 1901

Up at 8:30. Crew has been grappling for the anchor
chain. Gave it up at 12 noon. Placed a cache so as to
locate it next year. We picked out the walrus heads
this morning and the tusks. All had individual pictures taken by Dr Cook. We have 70 dogs aboard
and 20 Huskies, 53 walrus aboard, cut up, and a terrible mess and stink. Will take on 50 more dogs at
Nerkie. We were aground again this morning; getting to be a regular diet, so do not pay any attention
to it. Steamed over WeaukSua[119] Rock and there
Mr. Peary bought 4 dogs, 10 narwhal horns and
quantities of walrus line all for 8 barrels, 24 shells, 4
dozen ship biscuits, 1 Swiss knife. Started for
McCormick Bay but found it full of ice and impossible to get in. Marie [Peary] was born there [at]
Anniversary Lodge. Next place is Robertson Bay
for water and grass. Grass to be used in the
kamiks.[120] Mr. Peary gave each of us a narwhal horn.
—Bement

Walrus head as gift from Peary (B338)

---

119. Means "large stone" in Inuit language.

120. Fur-lined boots used by Inuit.

Weeauksua, or large stone (in Inuit language) (W222/B258)
Thought to have been left behind by retreating glacial ice.

Peary gave walrus heads and narwhal tusks. Saw records: Lockwood.[121]
—Wyckoff

FRIDAY, AUGUST 23RD, 1901
Up at 7:40 A.M. [Stopped at] Igloodehominy. Anchored. Church, Stone, and myself went ashore hunting. Church shot four auks, one raven, also wounded a blue fox but he got away. [It was] the only one any of us had seen. I shot five auks. Back to ship for dinner. Loafed balance of the day. Played chess at night. Had usual midnight lunch in the engine room. Turned in 12:30 A.M. The ground [is] covered with snow.
—Bement

After grass.
—Wyckoff

SATURDAY, AUGUST 24TH, 1901
Up at 8 A.M. Anchor weighed. At 4 A.M. on way to Nerkie. Found ship (Windward) and latched to her by 10 A.M. Transferred 30 tons of ballast, 50 dogs, 30 Eskimos, and any quantity of stuff for Peary. Took one of their sick firemen to bring home, also wife of the steward [Mrs. Percy].[122] The captain [Sam Bartlett] came with us as a pilot to show the way to Sabine. Reached Etah at 4:30 P.M. Strong head winds and rough sea. Landed the Husky's family and supplies belonging there. Dr. Dedrick went ashore with them. Just before he went, I saw him loading a shotgun, and asked him if he was going

121. Lockwood and Brainard's farthest north cairn of 13 May 1882, was opened by Robert Peary on 8 May 1900, and their records were taken by Peary for the archives of the *Peary Arctic Club*.
122. She was Josephine Peary's maid.

Playing chess (B89/W89)

Stone (left) and Berri playing chess while Bement (center)
and Bridgman look on.

Dr. Dedrick (left) and Dr. Cook (W105)

"It was a simple case of ordinary friction incidental to a voyage of such a character." (Dr. Cook, in Newark News, *16 September 1902)*

hunting. He told me he expected to find some hunting.

In about one half hour, a boat came alongside with two notes: one for Peary and one for Wyckoff. All of us were in the cabin and at once I knew something had happened. Peary made the remark after reading Wyckoff's note that it was a case for the doctor, meaning Dr. Cook; also for Wyckoff. Silence was then in order. Peary, Wyckoff, Dr. [Cook], and Berri reading. In Dr. Dedrick's note to Wyckoff and Peary, it stated that a letter for Mr. Bridgman would be found on the mantle. Mr. Peary's next statement was, "another Verhoeff case." Dr. Cook then said, "Can't we go somewhere and talk this matter over?" No lesser light. Took our departure to the engine room to think the circumstances over. Each one kept his counsel. Very little was said. My first thoughts were of suicide and found out afterwards [that] all of us had same thoughts. Dr. Cook came and called Wyckoff to the council. In about one half hour, Dr. Cook, Wyckoff, 4 Huskies and some dogs took boat to shore. They returned in about an hour, and after staying aboard for about 15 minutes or 20 minutes, started again. This time they were gone fully 2 hours and when they came back, we were all in the cabin again. Dr. Cook said that they had used all the arguments possible but of little use. He was bound to stay. By that time, out again the gang went but with a feeling of relief knowing he was all okay. Dr. [Cook] and Wyckoff took some hot coffee and packed off for shore again, giving us no information, but our

brains were working and we already solved the situation and waited for the details.

In about an hour, they came aboard again, this time to bring Dr. Dedrick. In the meantime, I had gone to bed but not asleep. Wyckoff came to me and said that Dr. Dedrick had resigned his position with Mr. Peary and was going to stay here another year alone, except for the Huskies, and asked my advice in regard to letting him have my rifle as he did not have any. I, at once consented and got up, getting what things I could think of to give him: 120 cartridges, rifle, darning cotton, gun cleaning rods, Hyomei[123] soap, candy. Rest of the boys gave him matches. Wyckoff gave him also 2 bowie knives. Dr. Cook [gave him] medicines of all kinds and offered him lots of stuff that he would not take. Some of us did. It was suggested that he be put in irons and by force made to stay aboard; but the Dr. [Dedrick] declared that he was not insane in the least, and we had no business to detain him against his wishes. In fact, [Dr. Cook] had told him ashore that if he did not come, he would force him to come. He climbed on an igloo and warned them not to try it as someone would get hurt; and said at first opportunity, would leave the ship by some means no matter where she was. Dr. Dedrick talked with Mr. Bridgman for about one half hour; and we all talked with him, but of no use. [He had] made up his mind to stay and as far as he was concerned, that settled it. So we all bid him goodbye and the Dr. [Cook] went ashore with him to try and persuade him to give in. Mr. Bridgman went to Mr.

123. Clarence Wyckoff was the owner of the Booth's Hyomei Company, which made soap and various pharmaceutical products.

Peary talks with Bridgman (W126/B53)

"Peary refused to talk to Dedrick and designated Bridgman to act for him." [Andrew A. Freeman, The Case for Doctor Cook. *(New York: Coward-McCann, Inc, 1961) 71]*

Peary's room and when he came out, called Wyckoff on deck. Soon Wyckoff came to me and told me that Mr. Peary gave us instructions to go ashore and get the gun and ammunition we had given the doctor [Dedrick]. Wyckoff told Bridgman that he very much disliked to do such a thing as it seemed as though it was taking the only means of support and his very existence from him and I objected on same grounds. Bridgman's reply was, "Then let him come aboard the ship or take the consequences." Orders were then given; when boat returned, we were to get the gun. But before it returned, Mr. Peary thought better of the situation and allowed the gun to stay with him. We feel better.

I went below to get warm and Bridgman came down and I commented on the awkward situation. And he took me up at once, on what grounds I sided. While we had done all in our power, except force to get the man to go, nevertheless, it would be a very hard thing to make the public at home believe we had. He remarked, who would know it? I said, everybody; I would tell. And all of us [would tell]. He said that he was not going to mention it in any of his dispatches or his paper so the public would not be any the wiser. And, furthermore, he stated that the doctor [Dedrick] told him that he wanted nothing said about it, whatsoever, at home. And that in his letters to his wife [he] had so informed her. But I said that the man will be back in a year or two and he is liable to stir up a dirty mess. Bridgman's answer was, well by that time it would be an old worn out story and I guess nobody will pay any attention to it. And then I said, I understand your wish [that] nothing [be] said when we get home. His reply was, "exactly." I heard

Wyckoff say to Bridgman that the doctor [Dedrick] had given him some letters to mail to his wife, and should he see that they were mailed. Bridgman's answer [was], "Yes, you take care of them." Wyckoff and I talked the matter over before going to bed and came to a few conclusions that would not look good in this book.
—Bement

[From] Igloo doo hominy to Kookan, [and then] to Nerke, while I was asleep. Picked up Windward at Nerke. Captain Sam [Bartlett] and his bowswain came aboard to act as pilot from Etah to Sabine. First mate Bartlett went aboard Windward to take charge and go and get Stein and Warmbath. Dr. Dedrick came aboard. Loaded ballast and dogs from Windward. Started for Etah and anchored late in afternoon. Ate at second mess tonight and during meal (Peary was sitting near table) steward brought in two notes, one for Peary, the other for me. Mine *read* as follows:

Etah, Aug. 24, 1901.

Mr. Wyckoff, Dear Sir:

I stated in writing to Mr. Peary, in my resignation, that if he did not accept my medical services, I would effect a landing at nearest possible point (where life could be sustained) to his headquarters. So I will remain ashore if I am refused acceptance at Sabine. I can reach Sabine latter part of November. I can live very comfortably with the Eskimos. I understand you had several rifles. Would you sell one and a hundred or two

Dr. Dedrick leaving the ship (W158/B52)

Dr. Dedrick (center) with two Inuit men, unloading while ballast (right) being loaded onto the ship.

cartridges and take my note, which my wife will pay promptly on presentation. If so, come ashore and talk it over. Please seal the two letters to my wife and mail to her by special delivery, or some way so they can be traced if lost; also mail the other letters (on mantel in cabin).
Sincerely,   T.S.D. Jr.

Please give this letter in original to my wife.

It seems that the doctor [Dedrick], after eating at first mess spoke to Mr. Peary and asked if he might go ashore with a shotgun and try for some hare. He sent gun and cartridges back by a native, also the notes and one hare. Peary, after reading his note, merely remarked that it was another Verhoeff case. We cleared out of cabin leaving Peary, Bridgman, and Cook to talk it over (Capt. Blakeney on lounge apparently asleep but really awake behind curtains).

After awhile I was called in and Peary told asked [sic] me to go ashore with Dr. Cook and try and persuade him to come aboard. It was decided if we failed (we were to use our own judgment) we were to use force if necessary—everyone (apparently) thinking him insane. I suggested that if insane we should get him on board with any kind of a promise and then forcibly detain him. This was agreed to. Peary showed me Doctor's [Dedrick's] letter in which he said he would not come on board unless he had a guarantee that he would be allowed to return to shore. On landing we talked with him fully an hour trying to get him to come. He absolutely refused. Cook appealed to him on his family's account, on his own account, and medical ethics—forcing his services where they had been

refused. I talked of responsibility if club would be held for anything that happened to him and we both exhausted ourselves talking–to no purpose. His one reply was that a doctor connected with an expedition should not retreat until the expedition did. He had resigned as second in command and would not work under Peary but as doctor he must and would stay, that he would not bother Peary or his Eskimos but would remain within cabin in case they needed medical assistance. His honor was more to him than life or anything else, and it compelled him to remain as near as possible to Peary's head-quarters. The whole thing appeared to me to be simply a quixotic idea. He did not impress me as being in any way insane and I did not feel like giving my word to a sane man that if he came aboard he could return (with the idea of detaining him). Dr. Cook evidently felt the same as he did not mention his going aboard, except that he should do so to see Bridgman (no mention of return to shore). Dr. [Dedrick] would not do it without guarantee. As a last resort Cook remarked, "Well if you won't come we will have to take you." Dr. [Dedrick] jumped up on stone igloo and remarked to Windward's bowswain (other oarsmen were Huskies) that he had better not mix with a quarrel that did not concern him, as he was liable to get hurt. Bowswain disclaimed any desire to fight. Said he had not come for that purpose; no fight. Dr. had been testing him. He would have fought to a finish, crazy or sane. Cook made a point of fact that when we landed, he (Dr. Dedrick) was sharpening pencil with Bowie knife and put same in boot handy. Dedrick said in talking to bowswain that he would not get stabbed. Finally Cook and I went aboard

Dr. Dedrick comes on board to talk (W148)

l. to r. Blakeney (standing), Moses Bartlett, Dr. Dedrick, Fullerton. "He received a new rifle and all the skins and furs he wanted, and then was accompanied to the shore, where it was seen that he would be situated as comfortably as possible—when one's abode is an ice hut—with a family of Eskimos considered very well-to-do in their tribe." (New York Times, *22 September, 1901*)

Herbert Bridgman reclining (B43/W162)

"Peary refused to talk to Dedrick and designated Bridgman to act for him. When it became apparent that Dedrick could not be dissuaded, Bridgman told him, 'You understand that you will not be given one ounce of food from the ship.'" (Freeman, The Case for Doctor Cook, *171*)

after talking with Peary and Bridgman (Cook made statement that he would not say he was insane now but thought Arctic winter might make him so). It was decided to have him on board (with guarantee to return him) so that Bridgman could talk to him. Done. Cook and I brought him on board. In my presence, and Cook's, he told Bridgman that he would not return on Erik or Windward, that club had none and need feel no responsibility on his account; that he could live with natives and if necessary, return via Cape York and whalers to New York. He would not interfere with Peary or Eskimos. Bridgman said if he did not return with us, he would forfeit bonus. He did not admit this. Bridgman made him hunt up the gun he had taken ashore and prove it was on the boat. Mr. B[ridgman] is a skunk.

When he went, we gave him 7 dozen boxes [of] matches, 2 Bowie knives, (1) 30-40 rifle (Louie's), 110 cartridges, 6 cakes Hyomei soap, and 1/2-pound Hylers [candy] (stuffed into bag without his knowing it). Cook took him ashore. My idea was that if [he were] kept by force, the fight would send him crazy; that he would jump overboard at first chance (he had told Peary he would do this). The best thing to do was to leave him. After he had gone, Bridgman came and said Peary said we must get back gun; that it was possible he might use it on Peary, and Peary and Mrs. [Peary] wanted it back. Peary said he wanted it and cartridges back because of trade and influence it would give him with natives. [He was] afraid he would have an expedition of his own *and get it.* Cook said [he] thought (after last talk ashore) he intended to go over Cape Sabine way hunting and try to make up with Peary.

The *Windward*
(right) meets the
Erik (left) (K1)

Dr. Cook (right) tries to talk with Dr. Dedrick (C24)
*" . . . for four long hours, with a cold Arctic wind playing up and down
our backs, we tried to get the doctor to return." (New York Times, 25
September 1902)*

Dedrick had told Bement he intended to get up
expedition to come up here. It is possible that he
would feel dishonored to go back before work was
finished. Would have no influence for our scheme.
Mrs. Cora B. Dedrick (7 letters to mail) T.S
Dedrick, Jr. Washington, Warren Co., N.J.
—Wyckoff

SUNDAY, AUGUST 25TH, 1901

Up at 8:30 A.M. Found ship surrounded by ice
varying from 5 to 15 feet thick but in large pans;
not a drop of water in sight. Cape Sabine in sight
but might as well be 1000 miles away. We have been
bunting ice all night. For two hours today we
squeezed and wormed fully 30 feet. We are
icebound in Erik, but nobody alarmed over the
possibility of wintering here. The shadow of the
Dedrick case hangs over the fellows. [I] overheard
Bridgman criticize Wyckoff this morning to Peary
on the gun question. Have not changed our opin-
ion of him. On the contrary have formed stronger
ones. Captains had a scrap on the bridge at 10:30
P.M. Captain Blakeney retired to the engine room
to cool off after Captain Bartlett took command.
We made from 11 to 12 A.M. about 400 feet. A bear
has been sighted by one of the sailors and we are
going to take up our regular watches through the
night: Wyckoff first 12–2; Church 2–4; Bement 4–6;
Berri 6–8; Stone 8–12.
—Bement

Did not get up until 1 o'clock P.M. and we were fast
in ice near Sabine. A year ago tomorrow the
Windward made into the ice here which same held
her for winter. Captain Sam Bartlett in command of

OPPOSITE: **Filling the water tanks** (B154/W132)

"We would run out a section of hose to a depression in the ice, where ice had melted and water had accumulated and would fill our tanks in this way. When we filled them up for our run home, one of the sailors carefully broke a hole through the bottom of the pool communicating with the deep sea underneath. This was done, of course, to avoid the constant moving of the hose from one pool to another. It did not improve the water in the tanks." (Wyckoff Notes)

Retrieving water for the *Erik* while she is fast in the ice (B202)

"The captain's way of landing a party on the ice was to run full speed and jam the bow into the ice so that one could descend by a ladder from the deck. I was out on a large pan with another member of the party when the captain started to land in this way and when we stopped running, the bow of the ship was right where we had been standing." (Wyckoff Notes)

Dodging icebergs (W348)

Windward had orders to land a cache at Sabine and make northward to communicate with Peary. Peary and Dr. Dedrick had not returned from north. Captain [Bartlett] had no orders to retreat so [he] tried to get north. [He kept] trying until fast in ice for good. [He] could have gotten out for a week after entering. This day [of the] week a year ago was last chance to move ship from position we are in. [The] two captains had a scrap. [There was a] man aloft conning the ship and Blakeney [was] on bridge, as is his usual custom as he was paying little attention to man aloft. So Bartlett took him to task. Blakeney finally went to bed after Peary talked to him.
—Wyckoff

MONDAY, AUGUST 26TH, 1901
Took my bear watch at 4 A.M. until 6 A.M. No bear. Very heavy snowstorm like we have home in January. Made about one half mile through the ice last night from 12 to 6 A.M. Did not sleep in, on account of the bumping and scraping of the ice on side of the boat. Poor prospects of getting loose of the ice for some days. All the dogs on deck are in very bad condition for fighting and exposure. At 5 P.M. we broke the pan of ice that was the key-stone; and that [has] held [us] back for the last 12 hours. All seemed clear to the headland. Made full speed for about an hour dodging between bergs and pans, scraping the sides, and just missing being pinched as the ice is moving all the time. We were out on the ice with ropes and ice anchors, axes and boat hooks, pushing, cutting and with the aid of the steam wench, escaped many a pinch.

At 7:30 P.M. the captain saw an opening between a large pan and a glacier, which discharged directly into the sea. There was just room for [the] ship to go through. So in we went, and scraped through except about 20 feet aft where the pan slowed and pushed us against the glacier and itself. It squeezed so hard that it lifted the ship out of the water, and gave such a list that we could hardly walk on the deck. Things look pretty blue. This is the first time I think any of us had thought of real danger—and in great danger we certainly were. So much so, that Mr. Peary went below and awoke Mrs. Peary and Marie, had them dress, and come up on the bridge. The ship groaned and squeaked under the pressure. We expected every minute her sides would go in. They got out a hawser on the ice and Dr. Cook, Church, Berri, and the Huskies and sailors, went on the pan to anchor the rope around a berg. And on the way over, Berri stepped on a piece of float ice and down he went. Fortunately there was ice under Mr. Berri [or he] would have gone clear under. Elway,[124] on deck, saw it and yelled to the men on the ice; but they either did not hear or could not make out what was wanted, and poor Berri had to get himself out. When he came aboard, he was a sight, but none the worse for his bath. Temperature of water 28°F.

They got the rope anchored and started the wench, and after a time, the ship moved, but it was by inches. It took 10 minutes by actual time to move 6 inches; but it counted, and it began to right after

124. Probably one of the sailors.

Marie Ahnighito Peary (W45)

"This is the first time I think any of us had thought of real danger—and in great danger we certainly were. So much so, that Mr. Peary went below and awoke Mrs. Peary and Marie, had them dress, and come up on the bridge." (Bement Diary)

The ship surrounded by ice six to thirty feet thick (w320)

"In every direction seaward, only impenetrable ice could be seen, and but a narrow channel of water like a canal, not enough with which to handle the ship with any degree of safety, was available."(Kersting, The White World, *196)*

Lecourt Point (B253)

"The ship was forced in a niagara of ice for fully five miles, at great peril sweeping everything before it." (Bement Log)

about one and a half hour's work. We got clear and out into about 2 acres of water where we anchored to the ice for the night and made repairs to the injection pump, with hope that the pan will not close in on us again. We are [within] about 5 miles of Cape Sabine where we are to land stores. The ship had a very narrow escape. It would not have been counted so if we had not been next to [the] glacier.
—Bement

Ice around us is from six to thirty feet thick. In trying to pass along the base of a glacier, the floe moved in and caught us fast. Stone and I were playing chess in cabin and when the ship listed over, we thought it time to go on deck. The ice came in Bridgman's port (from glacier). Berri fell in the water to his waist (hole in ice). [We] are in a little lake now. No outlet. During last 24 hours here, crew have seen 1 bear, 3 walrus, and seal. Peary says we have two weeks before we should worry. If wind doesn't blow from south (southwest) and drive ice away, we are here for good.
—Wyckoff

TUESDAY, AUGUST 27TH, 1901

Up at 11:30 A.M. Found conditions the same as last night. Engine all to pieces and no steam. All hands rushing work. Our position none of the best. At 12:30 the ship broke [the] ice anchor and got adrift. Got out double line and once more all okay for time being. [At] 4 P.M. the ice shifted and leads opened up. Made two miles and stopped by the flow. Mr. Peary started for shore to climb a mountain to see if there were any openings. [He had] just lowered boat and started when a big berg came down on them with the tide going about [a] 5 mile gait. They had a very hard time from being crushed against the ship, but managed to pinch through and started for shore. [They] had to turn again with close shave from another crush when the berg struck us. Up and over we went until you could hardly stay on deck. Inside of five minutes we were helmed in with ice, impossible to stir, and prospects worse than ever. Now it begins to look as if we were good for the winter. One good thing about it is that land is close by and we can get ashore. Also, the Windward is down on the outside of the pack [and] loose so it can take word home that we are all okay. Still she has not seen us for five days. We are drifting at 8 P.M. near shore one half mile. Have turned head on and if we go on the rocks, it will be bow on, with very little injury to boat. The question is how will we get off [the rocks]? At 10 P.M. a lead opened and we got off; 100 feet more after an hour's work.

—Bement

Lecourt Point two hours later (W135/B254)
Shows shadow of ship after she is forced up and onto her side. (Bement Log)

Ice. Ran into a glacier and the floe came to and jammed us. Peary called wife and child from sleep. Jammed over on side pretty well. Out and on ice.
—Wyckoff

WEDNESDAY, AUGUST 28TH, 1901
Up at 8 A.M. Found that we were fully a mile from the rocks, with any quantity of water to the east and south of us, but very thick ice and badly rafted to the north where we wish to go. Sabine Cape, Payer Harbor [is] nine miles away and in plain sight. Impossible under the present conditions to

get there. At 1:30 A.M., Mr. Peary gave up the idea of landing in Payer Harbor and dropped back to Lecourt Island, Hanseraq Harbor. Got into the harbor at 2 A.M. and anchored [at] 2:45. Mr. Peary took boat and started ashore to select place for camp and landing supplies. At 6 P.M. we started to unload the walrus meat, plus or minus 54 of them, and when they hauled over that mess, the stink was awful. It had been lying there for two weeks. Mr. Peary's personal stuff was put over aft. We all helped with that. Did not get goods landed until 12 A.M. The dogs caused great trouble as well as amusement to see the sailors rustle about the slippery deck with a dog. They let them down by the neck with a rope into a boat. Some of the poor brutes missed the boat and took an ice water bath. They were fighting on deck and in the boats. Hard time landing them. When they were turned loose to run, they took advantage of it. Turned in at 1 A.M. Helped at the wheel in harbor, helped lead boats to camp; helped put up tent.
—Bement

Gave up trying to get to Sabine. Heavy floes and pans. Several square miles in a single pan. Fifteen to fifty feet thick. Managed to get near shore in Herschel Bay. Decided to land stuff there, about 10–12 miles south of Sabine. Found deserted igloos here. Also deer tracks and antlers, and hare; probably musk ox inland. Landed all the walrus meat and dogs. Deck has been covered with meat since August 7 and in the twenty days has become putrid. The stench has been frightful. Got used to it and only realize how bad it was because of its absence. Had sixty or seventy dogs aboard and they howled day and night, and fought continually. Almost every one was raw in several places from bites and blows. They are fed twice a week. They were tied all over the ship in the meat and in the hold. Meat is dog and Husky food. Huskies go out among the dogs and pick up meat and eat it raw. This place looks bleak and desolate. Would hate to spend any time here. They will have to cart their stuff up to Sabine, after it freezes, by sledge.

Charlie [Percy], the Windward's cook stopped with Peary. Matt and six Huskies and their families comprise Peary's party. I gave Peary Louie's gun and 120 cartridges. Peary has given me a part of sledge runner he made north Greenland trip with. The largest root of willow he ever found, walrus tusks, one of [the] largest narwhal tusks known. [He] has seen one a foot longer than mine—small tusk. Has shown me [a] map of North Greenland made by him on trip. Highest he made was 83° 50'. Went down east side far enough to see mountain seen by him before from Independence Bay. Has named nothing as wants to wait and see if [he] discovers anything else; then club members get names on map. Peary is a thorough gentleman in every sense of the word. Nothing daunts him. Can stand anything and makes everything count for most. Believe no better man could be found for this kind of work. Lives as Huskies do and eats their food because can accomplish more. Will do anything to obtain end. Is a peach. Has talked as if we knew (from Bridgman) of his winter work and has made no secret of it whatever.[125] Bridgman is not social

125. Possibly a reference to Peary's fathering an Inuit child.

Ninety-six dogs, thirty Inuit, and crew all roaming the deck (B261)

"Blood from the meat was tracked all over, and the day before we landed, when the steward for the first time, washed the cabin floor we were amazed that it had a linoleum covering." (Wyckoff Notes)

Robert Peary with sledge (B47)

*"There is evidently an undercurrent of feeling on the ship that you are to
remain for the winter; that the Erik cannot free herself from the ice, and that
it will be impossible to go home. But I want to assure you that there is not
one chance in a hundred of this; under no circumstances will we take any
avoidable risk; we will stand by and work along the shore as far as possible,
when if we find that we cannot reach Payer Harbor, we will then land our
Eskimo, dogs, meats and supplies, in a safe and accessible camp, and I will
do the rest myself."(Peary as quoted in Kersting,* The White World, *196)*

Inuit family (B310) FAC

*"Every man and boat was set at work, and in two hours or less
the tents were up, the natives were on shore, and the beginning of
a booming town of the mining variety was visible; all the dogs
and all the meat were landed on the opposite shore and before we
'turned in" that night the greater part of the work of debarkation
was completed."(Kersting,* The White World, *197)*

Dinner on the *Windward* (B354)

*l. to r. Clarence Wyckoff, John Blakeney, Fred Church, Louis Bement,
Herbert Berri, Marie Peary, Josephine Peary, and Robert Peary.*

and so didn't talk. [Bridgman] is a slob and one time note shaver (told Bement so). Bement heard him say to Peary that he thought because of giving gun to Dedrick I was not serving club and sounded nasty about it. Peary shut him up; giving gun was like throwing crust to starving dog. Peary left ship for good [at] 2:15. Ship left after having been in Herschel Bay 24 hours.
—Wyckoff

THURSDAY, AUGUST 29TH, 1901

Up at 8 A.M. Getting little odds and ends together for last boatload. Everybody went ashore to inspect camp. They have a good camp and were fitted out. Took pictures, picked up stores, aboard again at 11:30.

Dinner at 12:30 and at 2 P.M. ran up the American flag and English flags. At 2:15 Mr. Peary, Matt [Henson] and Charlie [Percy] said good-bye to all.[126] As Mr. Peary went over the side, three hearty cheers were given by the entire ship and a salute of firearms and the whistle.

It was answered by Peary and his crew of Huskies. At 2:45 (just 24 hours) we raised [the] anchor and steamed with the ice again with no possible lead in sight. Just pushed our way through. From the crow's-nest, water can be seen about two miles to the west and if we were in it, would feel sure of getting out. All okay, bunting very heavy ice until 6:30 P.M. and got within a lead. We made a mile, but the ice is so thick, it looks like a hopeless job. We will get through it, I suppose. At least the captain

Women waving goodbye (C17B/B349)

Marie Ahnighito (left), Josephine Peary (center), and Mrs. Percy. "Mrs. Peary, on the quarter deck, bade her husband farewell, and then with the same self-possession and confidence which are a part of his nature, Peary himself went over the side and into the boat, amid our cheers and the volley of our rifles." (Kersting, The White World, *197)*

126. Mrs. Josephine Peary and Marie Ahnighito Peary stayed on the *Erik* to return home with the expedition.

Peary's crew (B297)

*These are the Inuit Peary took north with him. Matthew Henson is
seated in the center.*

says so. Have been going 4 hours and Mr. Peary's camp is in full sight. Struck an opening, which carried us about 4 miles more but ended; again heavier ice and small bergs. The bow of the ship got swiped between two flows and it took a lot of hard work to get out of the bad position. Turned in [at] 11:40.
—Bement

FRIDAY, AUGUST 30TH, 1901

Up at 8:30 A.M. Very cold out. Ice formed 3 inches thick last night in the openings. Found that we were very close to Greenland shore. About 8 miles away, making about 20 miles [that] we have come since 3:30 yesterday. Now [at] 9:30 A.M., we are in a basin surrounded by heavy flows. The longest bergs yet. Some are fully 2 miles long but not over 30 or 40 feet high. It does not seem possible that a ship of any construction, to say nothing of the Erik, could possibly come through ice as heavy as we have gone through in the past 6 days. Ice from 5 feet to 20 feet and bergs 30 to 100 feet thick and these we have pushed, pulled, and edged aside. This is the real Arctic ice. At 12 o'clock we cleared the ice. Into open water. Everybody felt relieved and thankful. Now on way to Netchiloomy to meet the Windward and return Captain Bartlett and his boatswain and get our first mate, Mr. Bartlett [Moses], and then [head] straight for Sydney and home. Glad to go, and dislike leaving this interesting country. Berri was seasick today, being quite rough and fair wind so set topsail. Made 8 1/2 knots for 4 hours. This expedition of ours has the distinction of being the longest stay north of the Arctic Circle of any that ever went and returned in one season, nearly 6 weeks. The sun is setting early

Herschel Bay where they landed Peary (B240) FAC

"Keep your flags up . . . until you are clear of the ice; we will see you through our glasses, and when we can no longer make out your flags, then we shall know that you are safely on the way home." (Peary, as quoted in Kersting, The White World, 198)

Returning to Cape York (B275)

Kaiotah, "kuna" (wife) and "mickininny" (baby).

[at] 9 P.M. Reached Netchiloomy. At 10 P.M. took Kiotie and wife, child, ten more dogs, to land at Cape York. [The] first mate [Moses Bartlett] was going to start out with the Windward Saturday morning to look for us; he thought something had happened to the Erik. We have been talking over the experience we had in the ice and came to the conclusion that we had a very narrow escape from being crushed. Also, from being caught for the winter. Left Netchiloomy at 11 P.M. for south.
—Bement

In ice. [The ship] ran up on pan. [It was] very nearly nipped but instead [the ship was] shoved off by ice coming together at bow.

Got clear of ice about noon and picked up Windward at 9 P.M. Mate Bartlett was just ready to start to look for us; thought we were jammed or wrecked. Temperature 27°, water 28°, ice frozen 3 inches.
—Wyckoff

SATURDAY, AUGUST 31ST, 1901
Up at 11 A.M. Found that we were among the bergs, and some pan ice head winds. Did not reach Cape York until 7 P.M., seven hours behind scheduled time. Landed Kiota, family, dogs, etc. Left them at 8 P.M.

Into heavy pan ice and quantities of bergs. The pans got lighter and lighter until we set sails and broke them like glass, being only from brick [size] to 3 feet thick. At 10 P.M. we cleared the pack and [we are now] in open water as far as the eye can see. All sails set and fair wind making about 8 1/2 knots. Expect to arrive at Sydney on [the] 10th of September. This is the first night we have had to light the clock lamp; getting quite dark [at] night.
—Bement

Arrived Cape York and let off Kiota and family. Getting dark nights.
—Wyckoff

SUNDAY, SEPTEMBER 1ST, 1901
Up at 7:40, back to bed at 8:30, slept until 12:00 dinner. Read until 3:30, slept until 6:00, loafed about deck between times. No ice. No land in sight. Nothing doing. Church's photo afforded great fun. Also Wyckoff's. At 12:30 A.M. I had a very severe attack of the piles; was up an hour. Suffered very badly.
—Bement

MONDAY, SEPTEMBER 2ND, 1901
Up at 7:30. Fair wind, cool, heavy swell, making about 8 knots. Opposite Upernivik at noon. Just see the coast, according [to] our position, about 65 miles off. Slept all the morning. Latitude 71° 58' 41" at noon. Longitude 59°. Taking observations now.
—Bement

TUESDAY, SEPTEMBER 3RD, 1901
Up at 7:30. Took powder bath, went on deck for wash. Bet the captain a bottle of wine that a certain fjord was the one we anchored in on way up. I lose, was ten miles out of the way. Wine to be served at dinner; $1.00 out. First cent I have spent in nearly two months; guess I can afford it. On deck in short pants and slippers. Fair little sea. I long for a big luscious, juicy, thick beefsteak.
—Bement

Burial stone of William Sharp (W246/B259)

"Sacred to the memory of William Sharp of H.M.S. North Star who departed this life November 1st 1849, aged 26 years."

OPPOSITE: **William Sharp burial site overlooking Mount Dundas** (W234/B260)

" . . . the body, fully dressed, is laid straight upon its back on a skin or two and some extra articles of clothing placed upon it. It is then covered with another skin, and the whole covered in with a low stone structure, to protect the body from dogs, foxes, and ravens." (Peary, Nearest the Pole, 338)

WEDNESDAY, SEPTEMBER 4TH, 1901

Up at 7:30 A.M. We are again in the ice but [it] does not amount to much. Crossed the Arctic Circle at 11 A.M. The captain celebrated the event by setting up a bottle of wine and Scotch whisky for dinner. Slept all the afternoon. On deck after supper. Grand moon. News getting rather stale.
—Bement

THURSDAY, SEPTEMBER 5TH, 1901

Up at 8:30. Sea has a heavy swell, which gives us a nasty pitch. Saw an aurora[127] last night, first time. Very pretty. Got into the ice again. Took some good bumps. Fooled the mate and watch last night by blowing into an empty bottle on deck and they thought it was a steamer whistle. Captain brought out the scotch bottle and we had highballs and a good time in general until 2 A.M. We have had a very heavy swell all day long, heaving things all about the ship. The largest swell yet, and strange that there is not a bit of wind all day. There must have been a great storm somewhere. Everybody seasick except Wyckoff, Church, Bridgman, and myself. I took a nap after dinner and at 3:30 was awakened by a crash. Found all the small articles in our cabin on the floor and when I got to the bottom, found my hourglass broken in a hundred pieces. Now I wonder what has happened? At 9 P.M. the swell still continues.
—Bement

FRIDAY, SEPTEMBER 6TH, 1901

Up at 7:30. Heavy swell still and no wind. Lots of icebergs in sight. Very large ones. Nights very dark and misty so cannot see the moon. Came very close to running into a large berg at 10 P.M. last night. Berri's 20th birthday and he set up a bottle of wine but he was too seasick to stay at the table. Mrs. Peary showed up for first time in two days.
—Bement

SATURDAY, SEPTEMBER 7TH, 1901

Up at 8 A.M. We sighted the coast of Labrador at 7 A.M. Coast very bold and quantities of small rock islands. Also saw a fishing schooner at 9:30 A.M. Did not speak as we passed by at 1 P.M.; sighted 6 more [schooners] in a bunch, all homeward bound, loaded down. Did not get near enough to speak. It commences to look like getting home. The swell continues but not so heavy. Wyckoff shot my hat full of holes today. Saw lots of whales. Church and Stone played Wyckoff and myself duplicate whist;[128] first cards played on trip. Everybody anxious to get in port. We are 1000 miles away from Sydney but all talk as if we were nearly home. Saglek Bay first point sighted in Labrador.
—Bement

SUNDAY, SEPTEMBER 8TH, 1901

Up at 7:30. Sighted number of fishing schooners at anchor in the Tickles[129] and took a bath at 10 A.M.

---

127. Aurora borealis, or northern lights.
128. A card game played by four players, two against two, with fifty-two cards.

129. Probably referring to area between Indian Tickle and Black Tickle along coast of Labrador.

Herbert Berri (W85)

Abandoned boat (C18B/B145)
"The captain sighted a dory dead ahead. It created considerable excitement; expected to find most anything from dead men up." (Bement Diary)

The captain sighted a dory[130] dead ahead. It created considerable excitement; expected to find most anything from dead men up. When we got along side, saw that it had broken loose from some fishing sloop. Had a lot of codfish, also all kinds of fishing apparatus. We hauled it aboard and found it a new boat, and [a] good one. In the excitement I lost my pack overboard.

Too heavy a sea to get it. The water tanks are giving out and we are short. The starboard tank is very salty and cannot be used. The captain is inclined to run in somewhere and get fresh [water] but Mr. Bridgman seems set on getting to Sydney regardless of consequences. He (Bridgman) is placing us in a bad position. In the afternoon we shot at porpoises, duck, gulls, etc. Saw whales. Everybody is getting a grouch on. [The] sooner we get to Sydney, the better it will be.
—Bement

MONDAY, SEPTEMBER 9TH, 1901
At last it [was] decided that it might be a good thing to get some fresh water as our tanks were nearly out. So we ran into Domino Run. Had a very close shave from going on the rocks; also from colliding with a big steamer that was there at anchor. Fishermen report fish very scarce. Caught cod off from stern by jiggers.[131] Anchored at 1:30 P.M.; raised at 4 P.M.
—Bement

130. A boat with a narrow, flat bottom, high bow, and flaring sides.
131. The lowermost sail set on a jiggermast.

Captain Blakeney (left) and Commander Bridgman (W24)

"We stopped at Domino Run . . . for water. As we came up to the harbor we had all sails set going before a gale of wind and making about 12 knots an hour . . . 300 yards from the shore we discovered that a ship was anchored across the entrance of the harbor and completely blocking it . . . the captain gave a signal to back the engines full speed, which of course, made no impression on our headway. The second mate had gone forward to repair the anchor and if that had not been ready, we would have had a most beautiful wreck. At the last minute, the first mate gave orders to let it drop. . . . Luckily everything held and we came up with a frightful jerk and swung around so we could almost jump ashore from the stern of the boat." (Wyckoff Notes)

TUESDAY, SEPTEMBER 10TH, 1901

Passed Belle Isle at 5:30 A.M. The large steamer, Lord Beaconsfield[132] from Scotland, passed us on [our] way to Montreal. Heavy gale struck us at 4 P.M., and continued throughout the day and night. Carried away three of our sails; strongest wind yet. Everybody is packing up. This headwind is keeping us back much to everybody's disgust.

—Bement

WEDNESDAY, SEPTEMBER 11TH, 1901

Gale continues. Dinky engine broke down again; fired in two hours. Such heavy sea that the wheel races about half of the time. The northern lights appeared again last night. Beans, salt horse,[133] coffee, and tea made from salt-water consolidation. Our fuse pretty rocky. Everybody disgusted and no appetite.

—Bement

THURSDAY, SEPTEMBER 12TH, 1901

Gale continues. Sighted Cape North last night. Expect to get into port Friday morning. Nothing doing. Everybody all ready to go ashore.

—Bement

FRIDAY, SEPTEMBER 13TH, 1901

Up at 6 A.M., and when [we] went on deck, [we] found that we were working up to the dock at North Sydney. First news we got was that McKinley was assassinated. We were a pretty blue crowd. It put a damper on our expectations. Bridgman and I went ashore at once to send the telegrams, get the mail, etc. Wyckoff and Church [went] to look up a carpenter. We hustled and got everything ready and said goodbyes, and started for the train. Got everything arranged and we were off at 11 A.M. for Carleton. Arrived at Truro at 6 P.M. and the party separated. Stone and Berri going to Halifax; Bridgman, Cook, Mrs. Peary and Marie for New York; us there for Carleton, by way of Quebec and Montreal. Got sleeper [train].

—Bement

SATURDAY, SEPTEMBER 14TH, 1901

Up at 7:30 A.M. First news was that McKinley had died at 2 A.M. Everybody offered their sympathy to us. The Canadians were extremely sorry. Saw flags at 1/2 mast along the way. Reached Quebec at noon. It was decorated elegantly for the Duke of York. Four ships, three Englishmen of war, and one

OPPOSITE: **Carleton Villa** (E6)

*Carleton Island, St. Lawrence River, near Cape Vincent, New York. Completed in 1895, it was a 64 room, five story, stone and wood structure built by Wyckoff's father, William O. Wyckoff. (*Thousand Islands Sun*, 23 August 1885)*

132. Named after Benjamin Disraeli, the first Earl of Beaconsfield, 1804–1881.

133. Slang used by the sailors for salted meat.

French in river at anchor, nearby. All flags at 1/2 mast. Stayed there for one half hour. Fine scenery all along [the] way. Reached Montreal at 6 P.M. Went uptown to wind down; looked about. Town looks quite American the way they decorate their city. Lots of flags at 1/2 mast. I saw several regiments embark for Quebec.

—Bement

SUNDAY, SEPTEMBER 15TH, 1901

Arrived at Kingston at 2 A.M. Found the Ezra Cornell[134] [yacht] at the dock awaiting us. Went aboard and started for Carleton. Reached there at 5 A.M. Folks all up and glad to see us. Stayed there until Wednesday, September 18th, and reached home on [the] 18th at 8:30 P.M. Thus endeth the finest and grandest trip any Ithacan ever took: no sickness, no accidents, [and] no cross words. Everything pleasant and the expedition accomplished everything it set out to do.

—Bement

Arriving home (E2)

l. to r. Church, Wyckoff, and Bement at Carleton Villa.

134. A 76 foot steam yacht belonging to Edward Wyckoff, the brother of Clarence.

WYCKOFF AFTER 1901

WYCKOFF AFTER 1901

Clarence Wyckoff, c. 1909 (P2)

On April 9, 1902, seven months after the expedition, Wyckoff married Maude Talmage, at the Washington, D.C. home of his bride's father, the world famous clergyman, T. DeWitt Talmage.[135] Talmage was a Presbyterian evangelist known for his thunderous sermons and fire and brimstone message. He published numerous religious books and his lectures and addresses appeared in magazines and newspapers throughout the late nineteenth century.[136]

Though Clarence and Maude had famous and wealthy fathers, privileged childhoods, and opportunities to travel the world, Wyckoff may have quietly agonized on the *Erik* over whether his own Unitarian beliefs could blend with such a religious family. In Bement's diary when he said, "Wyckoff wrote four letters; hardest job of his life. Been talking about it for 14 days," he may have been referring to Wyckoff's decision to marry Talmage. Herbert Bridgman, the commander of the *Erik,* in congratulating Wyckoff on his marriage wrote, "Dear Mr. Wyckoff, Really now, don't you think that in those dark days on the *Erik,* you might have told us this, and not made us believe that it was beans that caused your unrest of soul?"[137]

---

135. *Ithaca Daily Journal,* Wednesday 9 April 1902.
136. *National Cyclopedia of American Biography,* s.v. "Talmage, T. DeWitt."
137. Letter dated 10 February 1902, private collection, George and Bruce Pfann families.

The original advertisement placed in *Life* magazine, 18 November 1901 by the sales agency of Wyckoff, Church & Partridge (W393)

·LIFE·

Drive an Aeroplane

¶ The operating of an aeroplane, readily handled by the amateur, is now an assured fact.

¶ In the number of aeroplanes already purchased Europe is far in advance of America. This was likewise true with the introduction of the automobile.

¶ Our Paris correspondent writes us that hundreds of aeroplanes have been sold to private individuals in Europe. One manufacturer, alone, has sold 112—many of the early deliveries at large premiums.

¶ A substantial interest has also begun to arouse Americans. A great wave of enthusiasm has set in, and, although more different makes of heavier-than-air machines are to be had abroad, to America belongs the distinction of producing the lightest, speediest, and most practical aeroplane yet designed.

The Herring=Curtiss Aeroplane

amply demonstrated its supremacy at the recent Rheims international meet by winning the coveted International Cup, which brings to America next year the big world's contest.

¶ We invite those interested to favor us with a call. Americans desiring to enter the international contest next year should order machines early to secure prompt delivery, so as to be ready for the different events.

¶ A special inducement will be made to those ordering now for delivery after Jan. 1st, 1910.

Every HERRING-CURTISS AEROPLANE is demonstrated in flight before delivery to the purchaser.

Call or write to **Aeronautical Department,**

Wyckoff, Church & Partridge

1743 Broadway, at 56th St., New York City

It was Wyckoff's adventurous spirit and willingness to take risks that decided his marriage and landed him in various business ventures following the expedition. Wyckoff and his bride settled in New York City where he entered the automobile business with Alfred Church in the firm, *Wyckoff, Church and Partridge.* Together they started one of the first and largest automobile businesses in New York City.[138] From his showroom on 38th Street, he introduced airplanes to the American

---

138. Clarence Wyckoff, "Supersalesman '09: Promoter Par Excellence, Introduced the Aeroplane to Automobile Row," *Flying,* 1952.

public with the announcement of the sale of the first *Herring-Curtiss Aeroplane.*[139] Wyckoff also conceived the idea of painting taxicabs bright yellow and he operated the first fleet of taxicabs from his automobile showroom.[140] Wyckoff entered all of these ventures too soon, risked too much, and lost money in all of them.[141] He was very generous, putting many people through college, and helping to rebuild the Chi Psi Fraternity House at Cornell University when it burned to the ground in 1906.[142]

About 1912, Wyckoff returned with his family to Ithaca, New York where he continued to run the Booth's Hyomei Company.[143] He joined local organizations like the Rotary Club and became more involved in the community. Through his business, he had friends all over the country, but especially in the city of Ithaca who came to his rescue when his company fell on hard times during the Great Depression. His daughter, Betty, recalled when she became engaged to her husband, George Pfann, in 1929 that her father received a call from friends who offered to have her bridal gown designed and made by the Home Economics Department at Cornell University. Betty graciously accepted the offer.

By 1930, Wyckoff entered the life insurance field as a way of supporting his family.[144] He wrote about some of his experiences on the *Erik,* and he tried unsuccessfully to sell his stories to various publishers.[145] Wyckoff died in 1933, at the age of fifty-seven.

139. "Agency for Aeroplanes," *New York Times,* 27 June 1909.
140. Obituary, *Ithaca Journal News,* 31 August 1933.
141. Sisler. *Enterprising Families,* 89–95.
142. R. Charles Kemper III, "Alpha Psi History," *Sesquicentennial History and Biographical Directory of the Chi Psi Fraternity,* 357.
143. *Manning's Ithaca Directory,* 1912, s.v. "Wyckoff."
144. Ibid., 1930.
145. Essays and letters to various publishers, private collection, George Pfann family.

BEMENT AFTER 1901

The Bement Family, c. 1921 (B356)

Back l. to r: Lucie Panton, Ariel Bement,
Norma Bement. Front l. to r: Louis Bement,
Betsey Panton, Teddy Panton, Addie T. Bement.

BEMENT AFTER 1901

When he returned from the 1901 expedition Bement started his own business. He took over the Henry H. Angell shop located at 138 East State where he had worked for years, and he also opened a sister store at 404 Eddy.[146] "The Toggery Shops," as he called his new business, sold men's hats, caps, and shirts. Decades before catalogue sales became popular, Bement sold custom shirts by mail.[147]

Though not a graduate of Cornell University himself, Bement was said to have known more Cornellians than any other person not connected to Cornell because he had worked as a faculty messenger as a child. Following the expedition, he started a Register of Cornellians, and in many ways, this helped solidify his position as a fixture in Ithaca. When former graduates arrived in town, invariably they dropped by his shop, first to see "Louie" and secondly, to sign the register. Over the years, Bement collected names of graduates who became foreign dignitaries and Supreme Court Justices.[148] Many in his wide circle of friends, including the president of Cornell, asked him to speak about his experience on the

146. *Manning's Ithaca Directory,* 1901, 1902, s.v. "Bement."
147. Letters, private collection, Ayer family.
148. Obituary, *Ithaca Journal News,* 27 February 1933.

Erik. In return, they made Bement an honorary member of their alumni clubs throughout the country.[149]

Bement operated his business until about 1923 when he went to work as department manager for Treman, King and Company, a profitable hardware store selling everything from Ford automobile parts and tires to cutlery and cameras.[150]

It could be said that Louis Bement devoted his life to public service. Over the years, he helped to found and became a charter member of the Ithaca Reconstruction Home for Infantile Paralysis.[151] He was vice president of the International Society for Crippled Children and a member of the board of the New York State Association for Crippled Children. He became a charter member and past president of the Rotary Club. He also served as a member of the Protective Police, the Ithaca Veteran Volunteer Firemen's Association, the Savage Club, and the Town and Gown.[152]

The former dean of the Cornell Law School, Professor E. H. Woodruff, wrote, "There was no man in this community who for so many years won more gratitude from his fellow citizens for his unflagging helpfulness in every civic enterprise and in every personal need. By thousands of Cornell alumni of an earlier generation, he is regarded as one of the happiest recollections of their student days. He was ever optimistic about the future of Ithaca and the University and untiring in his spirit of solicitous helpfulness to his fellow men."[153]

149. Ibid.
150. Ibid.
151. Ibid.
152. Obituary, *Ithaca Journal News,* 27 February 1933.
153. Ibid.

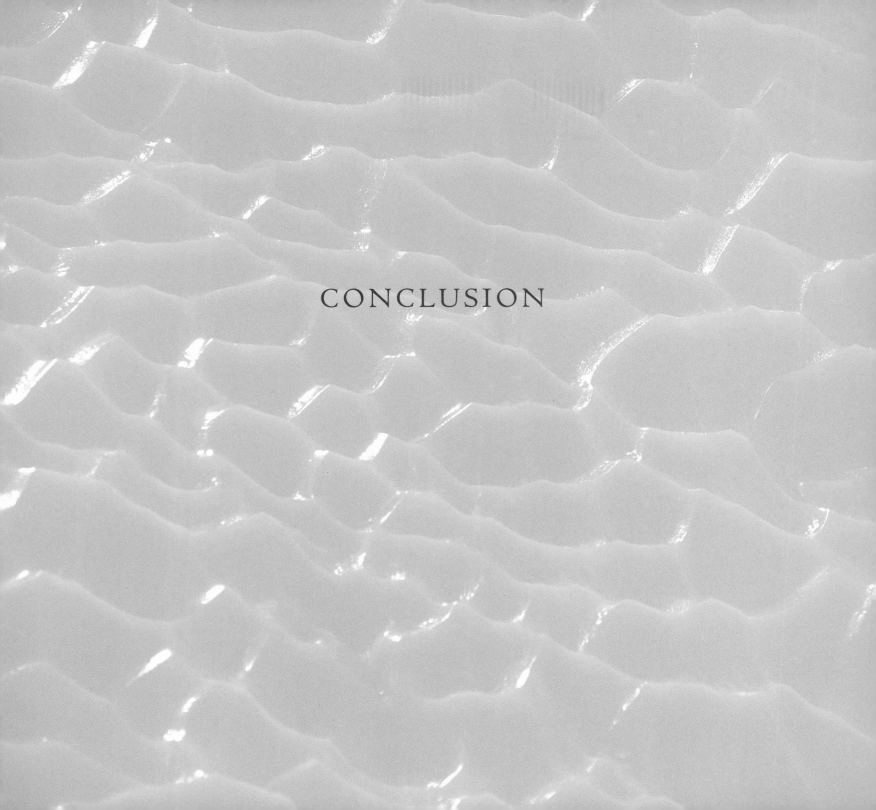

CONCLUSION

Clarence Wyckoff in front of musk ox
fur back drop (W66)

CONCLUSION

Following the 1901 Peary Relief Expedition, and particularly during the time when the North Pole became the focus of national attention, Clarence Wyckoff and Louis Bement found themselves in the glare of publicity. Everyone wanted to know what they thought of the two men who claimed they discovered the North Pole first. Captain Osbon, the secretary of the Arctic Club of America wrote to Bement, "I have read nearly everything that has been printed and am fully satisfied that there is a colossal conspiracy to down Cook which is bound to be a failure. There is no question in the world but what [*sic*] Cook is in the right and Peary in the wrong . . . There is more to come and when it does come it will be very damaging to Peary."[154] Another letter from Herbert Bridgman read, "why don't you get up and say what you know; that Cook never reached the Pole. It's fellows like you and Wyckoff and others who really do know, who keep this miserable fake afloat . . ."[155]

Wyckoff and Bement stopped short of openly taking sides in the Peary-Cook controversy. Wyckoff felt that Dr. Cook genuinely believed that he was the first to

154. Letter, 19 October 1909, private collection, Ayer family.
155. Letter, 20 October 1909, private collection, Ayer family.

Louis Bement in front of musk ox fur
back drop (E3)

the North Pole but he admitted that problems existed with the claims of both men. In a 1909 letter to Bement, Wyckoff wrote, " I still believe in Cook but not quite as strenuously as I used to. It is pretty near time that he began to do something to really prove that he has been somewhere."[156]

Dr. Dedrick corresponded with Louis Bement over the years, expressing his bitterness over his falling out with Robert Peary, but always mentioning his appreciation of the kindness shown him by Wyckoff and Bement. In a letter to Bement five years after the expedition, Dr. Dedrick wrote:

> Your letter comes to me like the cool music of ocean's roll lapping an iceberg. It took me right straight away from my desk where I sat fitting a woman with nervous prostration for glasses . . . took me to the "open," to the indescribable charm of the Arctic, to the heart corner where linger memories of men whom I almost love. You (and Mr. Wyckoff especially, of the rest) entered my life at the time when, though, if we never met again, you two could never go out of my life again.[157]

Sometime after the expedition, Wyckoff grew angry enough with Robert Peary to resign his membership in the *Peary Arctic Club*. The breaking point in his support of Peary involved a rifle and ammunition thrown over the ship to Dr. Dedrick when the *Erik* left the doctor behind in Greenland.[158] Perhaps because Dr. Dedrick signed a contract with Peary stating that everything resulting from his work belonged to Peary, the rifle turned up in Robert Peary's hands the following year. Peary donated it as his own to the American Museum of Natural History. When he learned this, Wyckoff became furious and insisted that Peary return the rifle immediately. Mr. Peary responded:

156. Letter, 8 November 1909, private collection, Ayer family.
157. Letter, Thomas S. Dedrick, M.D. to Louis Bement, 2 July 1906, private collection, Ayer family.
158. Although both diaries refer to the rifle thrown to Dr. Dedrick as belonging to Louis Bement, actual ownership remains unclear. The reason Wyckoff became so involved in its return has also never been explained.

Believe me I deeply appreciate the interest that you have felt in my work in the past and recognize the fact that you now have greater responsibilities. The rifle and ammunition which you so kindly loaned me a year ago last summer are now at the American Museum and if you will let me know where you would like them sent, I will have them delivered. The stock of the rifle I had inlaid with walrus ivory by Ahngoodloo at Payer Harbor last summer thinking that perhaps this might make the rifle somewhat more interesting to you.[159]

Eventually the rifle was returned. Wyckoff, however, never regained his high regard for Robert Peary.

Throughout their lives, Wyckoff and Bement remained grateful for their Arctic experience. When Louis Bement died in 1933, Wyckoff wrote, "When you are beyond the limits of police control, you learn to know a man as nowhere else. Everybody is apt to get lawless in such a situation. But 'Louie' was just the same there as on the streets of Ithaca. We encountered a lot of difficulties and dangers, but 'Louie' smiled through it all. He took everything as it came. He was always volunteering as a sailor or a hunter, for anything that needed to be done, just the same as he always has in Ithaca. He was joyous in everything he touched or did. He was the best friend I ever had."[160]

159. Letter, Robert E. Peary to C. F. Wyckoff, 4 December 1902, private collection, George and Bruce Pfann families.
160. Obituary, *Ithaca Journal News,* 27 February 1933.

BIBLIOGRAPHY

Manuscript Collections

Alfred Whiting Church Photograph Album. Division of
    Rare and Manuscript Collections, Cornell
    University Library. Ithaca, New York.

Edward Guild Wyckoff Papers. Division of Rare and
    Manuscript Collections, Cornell University
    Library. Ithaca, New York.

Frederick A. Cook Papers. Manuscript Division, Library of
    Congress, Washington, D.C.

The Dr. Frederick A. Cook Society Papers, 1891–1996. The
    Ohio State University Archives, Columbus, Ohio.

Newspapers

Evening (New York City) *Telegram*

Ithaca (New York) *Daily Journal*

Ithaca (New York) *Journal News*

Newark (New Jersey) *Sunday News*

New York Times

Thousand Islands (New York) *Sun*

Printed Sources

Albers, Patricia and William James. "Tourism and the
    Changing Photographic Image of the Great Lakes
    Indians." *Annals of Tourism Research* 10 (1983):
    123–48.

Anderson, Mogens Voigt, *Ilulissat-Jakobshavn, 1741–1991,*
    Illulissat, Greenland: Ilulissat Museum, 1991.

Anonymous, "Peary's Work in 1900 and 1901." *The National
    Geographic Magazine* 12 (1901): 357–61.

Berger, John. *About Looking.* New York: Pantheon, 1980.

———. *Ways of Seeing.* Middlesex, England: Pelican, 1972.

Berger, John and Jean Mohr. *Another Way of Telling.* New York:
    Vintage Books, 1982.

Boas, Franz. *Race Language and Culture.* Chicago: The
    University of Chicago Press, 1940.

Bridgman, Herbert Lawrence. "Peary's Work in 1901–1902."
    The National Geographic Magazine 13 (1902): 384–86.

———. "History and Field Work of the Peary Arctic Club."
    9th International Geographical Congress, Geneva,
    1908: 228–41.

———. "Ten Years of the Peary Arctic Club." *The National
    Geographic Magazine.* 19 (1908): 661–68.

Cartmill, Matt. *A View to a Death in the Morning: Hunting and Nature Through History.* Cambridge: Harvard University Press, 1993.

Condon, Richard G. "The History and Development of Arctic Photography." *Arctic Anthropology* 26 no. 1 (1989): 46–87.

Cook, Frederick Albert. *My Attainment of the Pole: Being the Record of the Expedition That First Reached the Boreal Center, 1907–1909.* New York: The Polar Publishing Company, 1911.

———. "The People of the Farthest North." *Everybody's Magazine* 6 (1902): 19–32.

Counter, S. Allen. *North Pole Legacy: Black, White, and Eskimo.* Amherst: University of Massachusetts Press, 1991.

Crawford, William. *The Keepers of Light: A History & Working Guide to Early Photographic Processes.* New York: Morgan & Morgan, Inc, 1979.

Elia, Susan D. "Chieftains." In *The Great Estates: Greenwich, Connecticut, 1880–1930,* by the Junior League of Greenwich, Connecticut. Canaan, New Hampshire: Phoenix Pub., 1986.

Frantz, Joe B. *Gail Borden: Dairyman to a Nation.* Norman: University of Oklahoma Press, c.1951.

Freeman, Andrew A. *The Case for Doctor Cook.* New York: Coward-McCann, Inc., 1961.

Gilberg, Rolf. Dagitkorssuag and Inughuit: Frederick A. Cook and The Polar-Eskimo. Paper presented at the Cook Symposium, Columbus, Ohio, October 1993.

Graburn, Nelson H. H. "The Anthropology of Tourism." *Annals of Tourism Research,* 10, no. 1 (1983): 9–33.

Greely, General Adolphus Washington, "Peary's Twenty Years Service in the Arctics." *The National Geographic Magazine* 18 (1907): 451–54.

Hayes, James Gordon. *Robert Edwin Peary: A Record of his Explorations, 1886–1909.* London: Grant Richards & Humphrey Toulmin, 1929.

Herbert, Wally. *The Noose of Laurels: Robert E. Peary and the Race to the North Pole.* New York: Atheneum, 1989.

Hoppin, Benjamin. *A Diary Kept While with the Peary Arctic Expedition of 1896.* New Haven, Connecticut, 1900.

Issenman, Betty Kobayashi. *Sinews of Survival: The Living Legacy of Inuit Clothing.* Vancouver: UBC Press, 1997.

Kaplan, Susan A. Introduction to *A Black Explorer at the North Pole,* by Matthew A. Henson. 1912. Reprint, Lincoln: University of Nebraska, 1989.

Kemper, Chuck. "The Cornell Fire of 1906." *Sesquicentennial History and Biographical Directory of the Chi Psi Fraternity* (1992): 64–69.

Kersting, Rudolf. *The White World: Life and Adventures within the Arctic Circle Portrayed by Famous Living Explorers.* New York: Lewis, Scribner & Company, 1902.

Laursen, Dan. *The Place Names of North Greenland.* Kobenhavn: C. A. Reitzels Forlag, 1972.

Lofgren, Orvar, et al. *On Holiday: A History of Vacationing.* Berkeley: University of California Press, 1999.

Lothrup, Eaton S. Jr. *A Century of Cameras: From the Collection of the International Museum of Photography at George Eastman House.* New York: Morgan & Morgan, Inc, 1973.

MacCannell, Dean. *The Tourist: A New Theory of the Leisure Class.* New York: Schocken Book, Inc., 1976.

Malaurie, Jean. *The Last Kings of Thule: With the Polar Eskimos, As They Face Their Destiny.* Translated by Adrienne Foulke. London: Jonathan Cape Ltd., 1982.

Munksgaard, Ejnar. *Grønlands Fugle* (The Birds of Greenland). Copenhagen: F. E. Bording, 1950.

Nash, Dennison. *Anthropology of Tourism.* New York: Pergamon, 1996.

Peary, Josephine Diebitsch. *The Snow Baby: A True Story with True Pictures.* New York: Frederick A. Stokes Company, 1901.

———. *My Arctic Journal: A Year Among Ice-Fields and Eskimos.* New York: The Contemporary Publishing Company, 1894.

Peary, Marie Ahnighito. *The Snowbaby's Own Story.* New York: Frederick A. Stokes Company, 1934.

Peary, Marie Ahnighito and Josephine. *Children of the Arctic.* New York: Frederick A. Stokes Company, 1903.

Peary, Robert Edwin. "Address On the Assembling of the Congress in Washington, September 8, 1904." *The National Geographic Magazine* 15 (1904): 387–92.

———. "Mr. Peary's Return from Greenland." *Journal of the American Geographical Society* 24 (1892): 470–73.

———. "Nearest the Pole." *The National Geographic Magazine* 18 (1907): 446–50.

———. *Nearest the Pole: A Narrative of the Polar Expedition of the Peary Arctic Club in the S.S. Roosevelt, 1905–1906.* London: Hutchinson & Company, 1907.

———. *Northward Over the 'Great Ice': A Narrative of Life and Work Along the Shores and Upon the Interior Ice-Cap of Northern Greenland in the Years 1886 and 1891–1897.* 2 Vols. New York: Frederick A. Stokes Company, 1898.

———. "Peary and the North Pole." *The National Geographic Magazine* 14 (1903): 379–81.

———. *The North Pole: Its Discovery in 1909 Under the Auspices of the Peary Arctic Club.* New York: Frederick A. Stokes Company, 1910.

———. "The Value of Arctic Exploration." *The National Geographic Magazine* 14 (1903): 429–36.

Reilly, James M. *Care and Identification of 19th Century Photographic Prints.* Rochester: Eastman Kodak, 1986.

Rosenblum, Naomi. *A World History of Photography,* 3d ed., New York: Abbeville Press, 1997.

Roosevelt, Theodore. "Letter of Appreciation to Commander Robert E. Peary." *The National Geographic Magazine* 14 (1903): 330.

Rosing, Kale. "The Greenlanders Past and Present," *Greenland.* Denmark: The Royal Danish Ministry for Foreign Affairs, 1951.

Sisler, Carol U. *Enterprising Families Ithaca New York: Their Houses and Businesses.* Ithaca: Enterprise Publishing, 1986.

Smith, Valene L. *Hosts and Guests: The Anthropology of Tourism.* 2d ed. Philadelphia: University of Pennsylvania Press, 1989.

Sontag, Susan. *On Photography.* New York: Farrar, Strauss and Girouz, 1977.

Stern, Pamela. "The History of Canadian Arctic Photography: Issues of Territorial and Cultural Sovereignty." In *Imaging the Arctic,* edited by Jonathan C. H. King. Seattle: University of Washington Press, 1998.

Takagi, Dana. "Racial Discrimination." In *Reader's Companion to U.S. Women's History,* edited by Wilma Mankiller et al. Boston: Houghton Mifflin Company, 1998.

Urry, John. *Tourist Gaze: Leisure and Travel in Contemporary Societies.* Theory, Culture and Society Series. London: Sage Publications, 1990.

Vaughan, Richard. *In Search of Arctic Birds.* London: T & AD Poyser, 1992.

———. *The Arctic: A History.* Dover, New Hampshire: Alan Sutton Publishing, 1994.

Wamsley, Douglas and William Barr. "Early Photographers of the Canadian Arctic and Greenland." In *Imaging the Arctic,* edited by Jonathan C. H. King. Seattle: University of Washington Press, 1998.

Weems, John Edward. *Race for the Pole.* New York: Henry Holt and Company, 1960.

———. *Peary: The Explorer and the Man.* London: Eyre & Spottiswoode, 1967.

Whitman, Nicholas. "Technology and Vision: Factors Shaping Nineteenth-Century Arctic Photography." In *Imaging the Arctic,* edited by Jonathan C. H. King. Seattle: University of Washington Press, 1998.

Wood, Forrest Jr. *The Delights and Dilemmas of Hunting: The Hunting Versus Anti-Hunting Debate.* Lanham, Maryland: University Press of America, 1997.

Wyckoff, Clarence. "A Caribou Hunt on Peary's 1898–1902 Expedition." *Arctic,* 5 no.3 (1952): 178–82.

———. "Supersalesman '09: Clarence Wyckoff, Promoter Par Excellence, Introduced the Aeroplane to Automobile Row." *Flying* (1952) Cradle of Aviation Museum, Garden City, New York.

INDEX

Numbers in italics refer to photographs.

Doctor Dedrick (W139/B81)

"Giving instruction to two Eskimo boys on the bridge of [the] Windward." (Bement Log)

Henson reclining on deck (W76)

"The lure of the Arctic is tugging at my heart/To me the trail is calling/The old trail/The trail that is always new." [Henson as quoted in S. Allen Counter, North Pole Legacy: Black, White, and Eskimo *(Amherst: The University of Massachusetts Press, 1991), 184]*

A young couple of ages 15 and 23 (B317)
"Moonface and his wife; he had bats in his belfry." (Bement Log)

"Old Mag," as Peary called her (B290)

"The expert woman of the tribe with a needle." (Bement Log)

Marie Ahnighito at the wheel (B33)

"Of course I do not forget the good times we had on the Eric [sic] even if the bridge on the Windward is small we now have the roof of the new deck house on which to play. I shall surely remember you to the huskies especially the girls (Don't let Mrs. Wyckoff see this)."
(Letter from Marie Peary to Wyckoff, 29 June 1902, Private collection of the George and Bruce Pfann families)

Encountering ice en route to Cape Sabine (W366)

"The ship groaned and squeaked under the pressure. We expected every minute her sides would go in." (Bement Diary)

Walrus head on deck (B336)

"The bird on board which . . . now graces my den." (Bement Log)

Robert Peary (W2)

"During the autumn, he expects to make an extensive reconnaissance of the interior and the western coast of Ellesmere Land, with a strong probability of discovering natives hitherto unknown to white men." (Anonymous, Peary's Work in 1900 and 1901, The National Geographic Magazine, *361)*

Library of Congress Cataloging-in-Publication
Data
Peary Relief Expedition (1901)
Boreal ties : photographs and two diaries of the
1901 Peary Relief Expedition / edited by Kim
Fairley Gillis and Silas Hibbard Ayer III.— 1st ed.
    p. cm.
Includes bibliographical references (p.   ).
ISBN 0-8263-2810-5 (cloth : alk. paper)
    1. Peary Relief Expedition (1901)
    2. Wyckoff, Clarence—Journeys, Arctic regions.
    3. Bement, Louis—Journeys—Arctic regions.
    4. Wyckoff, Clarence—Diaries.
    5. Bement, Louis—Diaries.
    6. Arctic regions—Discovery and exploration.
    7. Arctic regions—Pictorial works.
    I. Gillis, Kim Fairley. II. Ayer, Silas Hibbard.
    III. Title.
G743 .P286 2002
919.804—dc21   2001007706

Interior scans by Foto 1 Photographic and Digital Imaging, Ann Arbor, Michigan
Map by Carol Cooperrider, Albuquerque, New Mexico
Printed and bound by C & C Offset Printing Co., Ltd., China
Text set in Bembo; display text set in Centaur
Book design and composition by Robyn Mundy
Production assistant: Freddy Cante
Editorial assistant: Adam Kane

The stern of the *Erik* (B174)

"It is almost 1,000 years since Erik the Red first sighted the southern extremity of the archipelago, and from that time Norwegians, Dutch, Danes, Swedes, Englishmen, Scotchmen, and Americans have crept gradually northward up its shores until at last, through the instrumentality and liberality of the Club, its northern cape has been lifted out of the Arctic mists and obscurity." (Peary, as quoted by Bridgman, Ten Years of the Peary Arctic Club, The National Geographic Magazine, 663)